RESEARCH METHODS IN INDIAN MUSIC

RESEARCH METHODS IN INDIAN MUSIC

Second Edition

Najma Perveen Ahmad

MANOHAR
2002

First published 2000
Second edition 2002

ISBN 81-7304-348-5

Published by
Ajay Kumar Jain for
Manohar Publishers & Distributors
4753/23 Ansari Road, Daryaganj
New Delhi 110 002

Printed at
Print Perfect
Delhi 110 064

To

the memory of

Ustad Naseer Ahmad Khan

of Delhi Gharana

Contents

Preface to the Second Edition

The encouraging response to the first edition of this book motivated me to improve its quality further, before bringing out its second edition.

There is a growing literature in the field of the art of music and musicology that is exploring the rich cultural heritage of Indian music and analysing the relationship of Indian music with other systems of music. All such studies require sound research methodology for good quality empirical work and development of knowledge in the field.

The principal concern of this book is to make available to the students, scholars and teachers of music the basic principles and concepts, processes and steps, tools and methods, alternative designs and approaches for research that have been developed in related fields and are relevant for empirical research in music. Further, the aim is to focus on special characteristics of knowledge in Indian music and the methods that are specially suited for research in the field.

My students and colleagues provided the stimulus to write this book. They pointed out the need for adequate literature on research methodology, specially suited to the unique requirements of research in Indian music. I am hopeful that this book will meet these requirements and expectations to some extent, and will receive a positive repsonse from the readers.

In writing this book I have drawn on a vast amount of literature on research methodology and relevant sources of data collection for music. Therefore, I have a profound intellectual debt to the numerous authors who have enriched the field of literature on the subject by their contributions. I have also benefited from the insights and experiences of my colleagues. I feel a deep sense of gratitude to Professor Mrs. Sumati Mutatkar, who has always been a source of inspiration to me for improving my work.

I am thankful to Manohar Publishers & Distributors for their sincere efforts in bringing out this improved second edition of the book.

Faculty of Music and Fine Arts NAJMA PERVEEN AHMAD
University of Delhi
Delhi

Preface to the First Edition

Music, a performing art, is often perceived as a field of study in which there is greater emphasis on the development of skills and practice as compared to the theoretical aspects. At times there is a tendency to think of the two as dichotomous and not as aspects of music mutually supporting and enriching each other. Consequently, the development of theory and research in music, which strengthen the academic foundations of higher learning in the field, generally gets lesser attention than it deserves. However, there is an emerging trend in most of the institutions of higher learning in music to introduce courses in research methodology in the postgraduate programmes, doctoral level research requirements for teachers, and to encourage more empirical research in music. Besides, the growing literature in the field of art of music and musicology is exploring the rich cultural heritage of Indian music and analysing its relationship to other systems of music. All such studies require sound research methods for good quality empirical work and the development of knowledge in the field.

As a music teacher, who has conducted and guided research, I find that though there are a number of books available on research methodology in other subjects, there are hardly any which specially address the unique requirements of research in music. Students at the Master's level, and those pursuing the M.Phil. and Ph.D. programmes in music, generally feel handicapped by the lack of literature on research methodology suited to their course requirement, or for planning and working on their research studies.

This book has evolved from my experience of teaching a course in research methodology at the postgraduate level, as well as from my personal experience as a researcher and supervisor of doctoral theses in music. This work is a modest attempt to fill the gap in literature on research methodology of Indian music. The book covers not only the well-established concepts and methods of research, but also highlights the special requirements of research in the performing arts and music. Further, it explores the unusual and highly relevant sources of data collection that are especially suited for research in Indian music, such as the oral tradition in music, sculpture, painting, frescoes, and manuscripts.

The purpose of this book is to make available to the students, scholars and teachers of music the basic principles and concepts, processes and steps, tools and methods, and alternative designs and approaches to research that have been developed in related fields and are relevant for empirical research in music. Further, the aim is to focus on the special characteristics of knowledge in Indian music and the methods that are especially suited for research in the field. An attempt has also been made to identify the problems in conducting research, motivation for research, and the need for institutional support for encouraging research in music.

The first two chapters of the book explore the nature and purpose of research and examine the types of research which are usually conducted in the disciplines of social and natural sciences, and relevance of these to the performing arts and music. In the third chapter on motivation for research, the psychological, behavioural, social, and institutional factors that hinder or facilitate research have been discussed in the light of some well-known theories of motivation. The fourth and fifth chapters focus on the various aspects of research design, the alternatives available to researchers, and the specific requirements in the selection and formulation of a research problem. The sixth chapter probes the concept, characteristics and types of hypothesis and its centrality for research.

The well known methods of data collection and their relevance for research in music have been examined in the seventh chapter. The eighth chapter explores the unique sources that have been found specially useful for research studies in the cultural heritage of Indian arts. Many fascinating clues and insights are provided by such unusual sources.

The contemporary trends in research and data collection through the Internet and the World Wide Web have been discussed in the ninth chapter. The last chapter aims at helping research scholars and students in writing a research proposal and synopsis which is usually a requirement to initiate a research project as the first step for registration in a doctoral programme, or post-graduate dissertation.

The book is based on the cumulative thoughts, insights, experiences, and contributions of many scholars and authors to whom I am grateful. I am deeply indebted to Professor Mrs. Sumati Mutatkar who has always been a source of inspiration and guidance to me in my career and academic work. I am also thankful to all my senior colleagues in the Faculty of Music and Fine Arts, University of Delhi, for their encouragement and help in this work.

I am thankful to Mr. M.L. Saini, Librarian, and other members of the Library System, University of Delhi, for helping me obtain the relevant documents while working on this book. I wish to acknowledge my gratitude to Mr. Mohammad Haroon of the Faculty of Music and Fine Arts Library, University of Delhi, for extending all possible help in making available the necessary literature. I am equally grateful to Mrs. Chitra for her valuable assistance in many ways.

I express my appreciation to Mr. Anees Chishti for his kind help and support in bringing out this work. Finally, I am thankful to Manohar Publishers & Distributors for their keen interest and effort in the publication of this book.

Faculty of Music and Fine Arts
University of Delhi
Delhi

NAJMA PERVEEN AHMAD

CHAPTER 1

What is Research?

Research is the process of generating knowledge through scientific methods. It could be described as the art and science of exploration, enquiry, experimentation, measurement, data collection, documentation, analysis, and testing hypotheses. And also of developing generalizations and discovering the underlying patterns and principles that give insights into the laws of nature, human behaviour, aesthetics and other facets of reality thereby advancing the frontiers of knowledge.

Through knowledge research provides a perspective to the past and the present, and opens up new directions for the future. It converts facts and data into information, information into insights, insights into theory and theory into knowledge. It traces the underlying principles beyond the surface reality which enable the researcher to view reality in a new perspective. Research is, therefore, the creative art of generating knowledge through scientific method. Sometimes it proceeds from the abstract to the concrete in a deductive mode and sometimes from the concrete to the abstract in an inductive mode. The two modes are, however, not mutually exclusive. These are interdependent and interactive approaches in the development of knowledge.

It is essential for a researcher to be free from preconceived notions and the compulsion to prove his/her opinions. Instead the researcher should approach the facts and empirical data with the torchlight of a hypothesis, and even be willing to completely modify or surrender the chosen hypothesis to the compelling revelations from the data, and unexpected glimpses of reality. The important element in research, therefore, is not the methodology, hypothesis or technique. It is the scientific attitude, the open-minded approach, the inquisitive and questioning mind, and the ability to perceive beyond the common sense interpretations of observable phenomenon that differentiate scientific research from abstract speculations and inert knowledge.

It is well known that the perceptions of observable phenomena are highly elusive. It is only the acutely sensitive and sharp observations by inquisitive minds like that of Copernicus that could detect the rotation of the earth behind the illusory movement of the sun from east to west. Similarly, in the social sciences, humanities and arts the great researchers are those who have meticulously collected facts and given them new interpretations, or developed theories and discovered the underlying causes governing social, political, economic, aesthetic and other aspects of human behaviour. In this process they have advanced knowledge in their respective fields and discovered the subtle principles that enables one to understand the complex phenomena including the evolution, nature, and various forms and styles of performing arts in different civilizations and cultures.

In the field of performing arts in India, particularly in music, the traditions of systematic research have helped produce insightful writings and theories by scholars like V.N. Bhatkhande. Presently there is an increased scope for empirical research in these areas through data collection from primary and secondary sources, and analysis and inductive reasoning in addition to the already existing tradition of research and writing based on deductive reasoning.

Whereas the advancement of research has been of a high order in the fields of natural and physical sciences leading to great accuracy and predictability through experimental and other scientific methods of research, in the fields of social sciences and arts the methods of study have been relatively less vigorous. This is partly due to the complexity of the phenomena in these fields, and partly a lack of research tradition in these areas. The need for developing innovative and creative methodologies of research to suit the nature and requirements of these subjects is most critical for the advancement of knowledge. Currently, interesting and new approaches are available in the study of the social and behavioural sciences, and creative arts. The emergence of novel and creative methods of study are transforming conventional disciplines like history, sociology, psychology, economics, political science, and linguistics. There is a strong need for similar innovations to enrich studies and research in areas such as languages, literature, culture, fine arts, and music and the other performing arts. This would help explore the rich heritage in these areas through scientific methods that may lead to better understanding and advancement into new directions.

In this context, it would be useful to consider Prof. Moonis Raza's observation on the main shortcoming of research in India. He writes that

> in the absence of theory building on the basis of indigenous experience, there is a continual tendency to fill the conceptual vacuum by importing ready made goods from the glittering departmental stores of the developed world, particularly of its English speaking segment. . . . It can not be said that the situation has changed qualitatively in the recent past. Not rarely the Indian scholar still tends to acquire the character of a research assistant validating a hypothesis evolved in one or the other of the developed countries of West. This is generally not due to paucity of financial but of intellectual resources. Though there have been some pioneering endeavours to build conceptual frames on the basis of indigenous experience, they have been too few and still embryonic to be able to compete with goods from abroad. Import substitution, therefore, continues to be a major national task, not only in the sphere of economy, but also and perhaps more so, in the realm of the intellect.[1]

Authors and thinkers have attempted to define research and identify the characteristics and scope of methodical and scientific research. The views of some select authors on the subject are presented here. According to Crawford,

> Research is simply a systematic and refined technique of thinking, employing specialised tools, instruments and procedures in order to obtain a more adequate solution of a problem than would be possible under ordinary means. It starts with a problem, collects data or facts, analyses these critically, and reaches decisions based on the actual evidence. It involves original work instead of mere exercise of personal opinion. It evolves from a genuine desire to know rather than a desire to prove something. It is quantitative, seeking to know not only what but how much, and measurement is, therefore, a central feature of it.[2]

In the opinion of W.S. Monroe,

> Research may be defined as a method of studying problems whose solutions are to be derived partly or wholly from facts. The facts dealt with in research may be the statements of opinion, historical facts, those contained in records and reports, the result of tests, answers to questionnaires, experimental data of any sort, and so forth. The final

purpose of educational research is to ascertain principles and develop procedures for use in the field of education, therefore it should conclude by formualting principles or procedures. The mere collection and tabulation of facts is not research, though it may be preliminary to it or even a part thereof.[3]

Neil J. Salkind defines research as

a process through which new knowledge is discovered. Theories are an important part of science. It is at the ground floor level, however, that the researcher works to get the ball rolling, adding a bit of new insight here and a new speculation there, until it comes together to form a corpus of knowledge. . . . A high quality research is characterized by many different attributes: 1. It is based on the work of others. 2. It can be replicated. 3. It is generalizable to other settings. 4. It is based on some logical settings. 5. It is doable. 6. It generates new questions or is cyclical in nature. 7. It is incremental. 8. It is an apolitical activity that should be undertaken for the betterment of society.[4]

According to P.M. Cook, 'Research is an honest, exhaustive, intelligent searching for facts and their meanings or implications with reference to a given problem. The findings of a given piece of research should be an authentic verifiable contribution to the knowledge in the field studies.'[5]

D. Slesinger and M. Stephenson define research as 'the manipulation of things, concepts or symbols for the purpose of generalizing to extend, correct or verify knowledge whether that knowledge aids in construction of theory or in the practice of an art'.[6]

On the subject of research Kettering expresses interesting ideas. In his opinion,

Research is a high-hat word that scares a lot of people. It needn't. It is rather simple. Essentially, it is nothing but a state of mind—a friendly, welcoming attitude towards change. Going out to look for change, instead of waiting for it to come. Research, for practical men, is an effort to do things better and not to be caught asleep at the switch. The Research State of mind can apply to anything. It is the problem-solving mind as contrasted with the let well enough alone mind. It is the composer mind, instead of fiddler mind, it is the 'tomorrow' mind, instead of the 'yesterday' mind.[7]

Keeping in view the above definitions of research, it may be stated that the function of research is to solve a problem, which leads to new knowledge, using methods of enquiry which at a given time are accepted as adequate in a given subject. The final purpose of research is to ascertain principles for developing a theory. The testing of its validity is not possible but for research. Hence research is often defined as 'scientific thinking' and an art of scientific investigation. Research is thus an original contribution to the existing stock of knowledge through objective and systematic methods of finding the solution to a problem.

Purpose of Research

The main purpose of research is enlightenment of the human mind, and to find out hidden truths which have not been discovered as yet. 'The purpose of research is to discover answers to questions through the application of scientific proceedings. These procedures have been developed in order to increase the likelihood that the information gathered would be relevant to the question asked and will be reliable and unbiased.'[8] The objective of most research is advancement of knowledge, irrespective of the fact whether a researcher is activated by motives of curiosity or of a practical nature. Usually it is not known in advance whether a research project will be useful or not, and if it will add to human knowledge or not. Thus it was purely a research motive which led Newton to inquire into nature and labour so patiently to determine the precise departure of the moon's orbit from a tangential course. The satisfaction in view was not primarily that of Newton's intellectual pleasure of knowing the precise curve, but of testing his hypotheses of universal gravitation. This knowledge gained by Newton was of immense value to humanity.[9]

In any type of research the objective is finding out facts of a phenomenon, individual, or a situation, and drawing inferences or generalizations which are based on logic and are convincing. Knowledge without logic and conviction is incomplete, and for a proper appreciation of the nature and content of research a thorough understanding of the scientific method is absolutely essential.

Though each research study has its own specific purpose, research objectives can be divided under the following broad groupings:

1. To gain familiarity with a phenomenon, or to achieve new insights into it (studies conducted with this object in view are termed as exploratory or formulative research studies).
2. To portray accurately, the characteristics of a particular individual, situation or a group (such studies are known as descriptive research studies).
3. To determine the frequency with which something occurs or with which it is associated with something else (such studies are known as diagnostic research studies).
4. To test a hypothesis of a causal relationship between variables (such studies are known as hypotheses-testing research studies).

Research, depending on it main objectives, can be classified into two categories: (i) basic or pure, and (ii) applied.

The main objective of basic research is the pursuit of knowledge solely for its own sake. It has little concern for the application of the findings or its utility to society. The basic or pure researcher is essentially interested in increasing his knowledge in a field of enquiry where many questions remain unanswered. The primary concern is the formulation of a theory or a contribution to the existing body of knowledge. To such a researcher knowledge and truth are of supreme value, and all else is secondary and subordinate. Such researchers are often described as fundamental researchers.

The development of the Theory of Relativity by Einstein and other scientific breakthroughs leading to an understanding of the fundamental forces, governing the physical, biological and other natural phenomena are examples of fundamental or pure research.

Applied research is directed towards the solution of immediate, specific and practical problems. Its purpose is to improve a product or process, testing theoretical concepts in actual problem situations. It has only a secondary position as far as scientific knowledge is concerned. Its main interest is in solving a specific problem here and now. Moreover, its findings are evaluated in terms of local applicability and not in terms of universal validity. The present day emphasis on operations research in industry and on action research in education is an outgrowth of the need for empirical solutions to problems in the immediate situation. Most research in the field of education is applied research, for it attempts to develop generalizations about the teaching-learning process and instructional materials. Educational research is concerned with the development and testing of theories of student behaviour in an educational setting.[10]

According to W.T. Adiseshiah, it is of utmost importance that the research investigator is fully aware of the purposes to be served by the research undertaken. A distinction has to be made between fundamental or pure research and aimed or applied research. Pure or fundamental research involves investigation of problems in order to further and develop existing knowledge. The object here would be to know precisely and exactly what happens in the course of a given set of natural events. In the case of applied or aimed research, the objective is considerably more specific and practically oriented. In this category of research, interest centres around a result which is useful.[11]

Since the major purpose of research is creation of new knowledge and advancing the frontiers of existing knowledge, authors such as T.S. Wilkinson feel that knowledge may be used for construction of a theory or the practice of an art. In their opinion the extended, corrected and verified knowledge has two possible uses: (a) theoretical and (b) practical.

Knowledge may be organized into propositions, and these propositions may then be meaningfully articulated to form a more abstract conceptual system affording estimations about a class of things or phenomena under specified sets of conditions. Such a use of knowledge is often known as theory-oriented and the activities of a scientist who seeks knowledge for the sake of building theories of 'non-utilitarian' import are often known as 'pure', 'basic', or theoretical research. Knowledge, on the other hand, may be used as a means to some practical or utilitarian goal, not just as an end in itself. The researches which seek knowledge mainly for using it to serve some practical ends, are often called 'applied' or 'practice-oriented'. One should not consider these orientations as a perfect dichotomy. There is nothing so practical as a good theory and the endeavours to solve practical problems have often given birth to theories. That is, practice is a blessing for the development of theory.[12]

Types of Research

Research studies can be classified into various types based on the nature of the study, the type of data and method of analysis, the general approach followed in conducting it, the time dimension relating the study and the basic development of knowledge. We shall now examine the different types of research studies, which are being generally utilized by researchers.

Historical Research

Historical Research has been described as the critical examination of past events or happenings in order to know the generalizations and the facts on which they are based. These researches are based on the premise that a proper study of the past will provide a key to the present. And also help in documenting the depth of knowledge based on the past efforts and contemporary state of knowledge in a given subject. It utilizes historical sources such as documents, archaeological and other evidences to study events, experiences and ideas of the past including culture and philosophy. An important and informative method of research, it is relevant for all types of researches, especially in the field of anthropology, history, the performing arts including music, and fine arts.

Historical Research either relates past events to one another or to current events. In fact like any other researcher, the historian collects data, analyses them, and then comes to conclusions about the tenability of his/her hypotheses. One significant difference between historical and other types of research is the type of data collected and the method of collection. Researchers involved in this type of research often accomplish this goal through the use of primary sources (original documents or people who have personally experienced an event), and secondary sources (second hand documents or people who may have some knowledge about the event but did not experience it first hand). However, even if these sources are readily available, one of the greatest challenges in undertaking such research is in assessing the accuracy of the sources.[13]

Descriptive Research

Descriptive research refers to collection of data and surveys pertaining to any contemporary phenomenon, such as opinion surveys or questionnaire-based surveys, field observations, and first-hand narrative based on direct experience (through 'Participant Observer' method). The objective of descriptive research is to ascertain the state of affairs as it exists at a particular point of time. This method is helpful in understanding existing patterns in the realms of social and natural sciences based on a variety of survey methods, which may also include comparative and co-relational approaches.

This form of research is often utilized in understanding cultural and social phenomena in a large number of studies. Such researches often provide a useful foundation for analytical and comparative studies and provide useful insights and documentations of the contemporary state of affairs in any sphere of life. In other words, descriptive research provides a picture of events that are currently happening or have occurred in the past and it often indicates as to how two or more things are related to one another, or how well a specific outcome might be predicted by one or more of the given pieces of information.[14]

Ex Post Facto Research

This research method refers to the study of events or situations which have already occurred and which are analysed by the researcher in order to understand the possible cause and effect relationship. In such studies the researcher has no control over the factors and variables influencing the situation or event. He/she can only report on what has happened or what is happening. For example, the major social and political upheavals of the past or those taking place currently can be studied under this type of research. These studies also include attempts by researchers to establish causes of events even though they have no control over the variables.

According to C.R. Reddy,

> In this type of research, the researcher has no control over the independent variable, more than this randomisation is not possible, which means he takes things as they are and tries to extricate them. One of the difficulties about which the researcher has to be careful and cautious is with regard to interpretation of data and drawing conclusions, since the Ex Post Facto Research is conducted without hypothesis and without prediction.[15]

However, since all research investigations proceed on some tacit, if not explicit hypothesis, the ex post facto researches can yield useful insights and findings for future research.

Analytical Research

Analytical research utilizes existing and available information and data for a critical analysis with the objective of discovering patterns, insights and generalizations that may help in building a theory or a better understanding of the existing phenomenon. An example of such research would be a study of the trends and changes in the demographic and sociological aspects based on an analysis of the census data.

Experimental Research

This form of research is generally used in scientific research in subjects like physics, chemistry, biology, psychology, etc., in which it is possible to control the variables and study the effects of changes in some variables in the laboratory or field situations. According to some authors it involves a procedure for gaining knowledge by collecting new or fresh observations under controlled conditions. Further, it reveals the causal relations and interactions. Hence it calls for precision and accurate observations. In experimental research independent as well as dependent variables are involved where the former can be manipulated as an experimental variable in order to see the effect on the latter.

It can also be called an empirical type of research, which is data-based and provides conclusions, that can be verified by observation or experiment. In such a research, it is necessary to get facts first-hand, at their source and to manipulate certain things to stimulate the production of the desired information. Evidence gathered through experiments or empirical studies is today considered to be the most powerful support possible for a given hypothesis.[16]

Greenwood suggests that an experiment is the proof of a hypothesis, which seeks to hook up two factors into a causal relationship. It requires the study of contrasting situations in which all factors have been controlled except the one that is of interest, the latter being either the hypothetical cause or the hypothetical effect. The basic factor in the case of the experimental method is the control over the subject of study and manipulation of an independent variable. It is not so much the control as such, but the degree of control in social experiments about which there are a wide variety of opinions.[17] The only way to establish a true link between cause and effect in any study is to isolate and eliminate all the factors that might be responsible for a particular outcome and test only those that you directly want to measure. Participants in experimental research are assigned to groups based on some selected criterion often called the treatment variable. The distinction between experimental and other methods of research does boil down to a matter of control. True experimental research designs isolate, and control, all factors that could be responsible for any effects except the one of most interest.[18] Examples of such research include trials of new drugs by pharmaceutical companies or impact of certain conditions on human health or disease in the medical field.

Pure and Applied Research

As discussed earlier briefly, one well accepted method of classifying research is according to its purpose, whether it is conducted to create knowledge for its own sake or for finding a solution to a given problem.

According to Hogben,

> Pure Research is not hampered by considerations of the social use to which discoveries may be put. It is interested first of all in the continuity and integrity of the thought process in science and philosophy. It permits the thinking process to lead where it will, no matter what erratic angle of direction is indicated. Pure Research watches the problem bud out in

terms of more or less likely hunches about other problems and other hypotheses. It listens to the suggestion of the insight. On the other hand, Practical (applied) Research must find its problem first of all on the present level of social procedure. It must deal with existent social status and always with the direct purpose of improving present practice. If Practical Research is not able to announce some economically valuable discovery within a reasonable time, it fails.[19]

J.R. Angell is of the opinion that an essential similarity in the so-called pure and practical research studies is that both use the scientific method of reflective thinking, although they have different objectives. The aim of pure research is not found in the realm of specific human need. On the contrary, the problems of applied research always involve some definite issue in experience.[20] Similarly, Neil J. Salkind believes that sometimes distinctions need to be made not only about the type of research but also about the most general category into which the implication or utility of the research might fall. This is where the distinction between basic and applied research becomes apparent. But this distinction is sometimes used as a convenient way to classify research activity rather than to shed light on the intent or purpose of the researcher and importance of the study. According to him the most basic distinction between the two is that basic research (or pure research) has no immediate application at the time it is completed, whereas applied research does. If this appears to be a somewhat ambiguous distinction, it is due to the fact that almost all basic research eventually, in the long run, results in some worthwhile application. Therefore, we must not judge the quality of either the finished product or the worth of supporting a research project by branding it as basic or applied research. Rather we should look closely at its content and judge it on its merit.[21]

Fundamental Research

In scientific disciplines a distinction is often made between fundamental and applied research. Fundamental research refers to the exploration of knowledge for its own sake at a very deep level without relating it to any immediate problem or requirement.

Action Research

Action research is the process of systematically collecting research data about an ongoing system relative to some objective, goal or need of that system. And involves feeding these data back into the system, taking actions by altering selected variables within the system based both on the data and on hypothesis, and evaluating the result of actions by collecting more data. Action Research is a process which works in two different ways. It is a sequence of events and activities: sometimes treating the same problem through several cycles and sometimes moving to different problems in each cycle. Both aspects point towards the ongoing nature of action research.[22]

The key elements in action research include problem identification, data gathering, diagnosis, and feedback to the client group leading to action planning and action. This sequence is repeated after action has been taken to further improve the problem solving ability and to evolve new solutions for the problems emerging a cyclical sequence. The client group as well as the researcher work and learn together in this process.

Action research may also be defined as the application of the scientific method of fact finding and experimentation to practical problems requiring action solutions, and involving the collaboration and cooperation of scientists, practitioners and laymen. It is a research which is inextricably linked to action. Furthermore, it is research-with-a-purpose, that is to guide present and future action.[23]

This type of research is utilized for facilitating change and development in a social system, like an institution or an organization. For example, it could help a small or large community, living in a specific locality, village or town, including individuals and groups, to overcome and cope with their psychological, social, economic or health problems.

NOTES

1. Moonis Raza, 'Geographical Research', in B.C. Tandon, *Research Methodology in Social Sciences,* Chaitanya Publishing House, Allahabad, 1987, p. 265.
2. See F.L. Whitney, *The Elements of Research,* Prentice Hall, Inc., New York, 1954, p. 21.

3. Ibid., p. 21.
4. N.J. Salkind, *Exploring Research,* Prentice Hall, New Jersey, 1991, p. 3.
5. F.L. Whitney, op. cit., p. 21.
6. D. Slesinger and M. Stephenson, *The Encyclopaedia of Social Sciences* (15 vols.), edited by E.R.A. Seligman, Vol. IX, Macmillan, New York, 1930.
7. C.F. Kettering, 'More Music Please, Composers'! *Saturday Evening Post,* 211: 32, 1938, p. 32.
8. C. Selltiz, M. Jahoda, M. Deutsch and S.W. Cook, *Research Methods in Social Relations,* Holt, Rinehart and Winston, Inc., USA, 1961, p. 2.
9. Q.H. Farooqui, *Logic of Research;* B.C. Tandon, op. cit., p. 67.
10. G.N.P. Srivastava, *Advanced Research Methodology,* Radha Publications, New Delhi, 1994, pp. 5-6.
11. W.T. Adiseshiah and S. Sekhar, *Educational and Social Research,* Velan Pathippagam, Coimbatore, 1977, p. 6.
12. T.S. Wilkinson and P.L. Bhandarkar, *Methodology and Technique of Social Research,* Himalaya Publishing House, Bombay, 1979.
13. N.J. Salkind, op. cit., p. 12.
14. Ibid.
15. C.R. Reddy, *Research Methodology in Social Sciences,* Daya Publishing House, Delhi, 1987, p. 12.
16. C.R. Kothari, *Research Methodology, Methods and Techniques,* Wiley Eastern Ltd., New Delhi, 1985, p. 5.
17. K.G. Gangrade, *Empirical Methods, Research Methodology;* B.C. Tandon, op. cit., pp. 13-14.
18. N.J. Salkind, op. cit., pp. 13-14.
19. F.L. Whitney, op. cit., p. 25.
20. J.R. Angell, *Proceedings,* Association of American Universities, University of Chicago Press, Chicago, 1919, pp. 27-8.
21. N.J. Salkind, op. cit., pp. 14-15.
22. W.L. French and C.H. Bell, *Organisation Development,* Prentice-Hall of India Pvt. Ltd., New Delhi, 1983, pp. 88-9.
23. Ibid., pp. 90-1.

CHAPTER 2

Research Process

The term research process refers to the key elements or steps required for a study, their normal sequence and inter-relatedness in achieving the desired objectives of a research project. Although there are many variations in the research process depending on the research design, there are broad similarities among most research studies. The major steps in a study consist of the following: identification of the problem, development of a suitable research design, formulation of hypotheses or tentative propositions, selection of the sample, methods and instruments of data collection, collection of data through primary and secondary sources, analysis and interpretation of the data, and testing of the hypotheses and propositions. These lead to findings and conclusions of a research study, which are presented in the form of a report. It may, however, be noted that although these steps are discrete and identifiable, and may be sequential, due to the high level of interdependence among the steps and the complexity of research, the process does not follow a linear pattern. The researcher has to anticipate the later steps well in advance and constantly make adjustments as the research proceeds, because of which a linear pattern does not necessarily follow.

In a sense, the process may be described as an iterative spiral. Although there are discrete logical steps which appear to be sequential in nature, such as definition of the problem, formulation of hypothesis, determination of sample, collection of data and its analysis, different elements or steps in the research process may have to be re-examined and modified in the light of subsequent developments and practical problems in the conduct of the study. Since the process is of a dynamic nature it requires flexibility and tentativeness on the part of the researcher to cope with the unanticipated and complex realities encountered during various stages in the search for knowledge.

This of course, does not mean a change in the basic objective or the fundamental problem that a researcher is seeking to address. However, as the work proceeds the researcher often discovers that the scope of the study is too wide or that the problem has not been thoroughly defined or the fact that data on the chosen subject is either not available, or is extremely difficult to collect and reduce to measurable categories. Similarly, the literature survey and fieldwork may bring to light new dimensions of the problem which may be more meaningful than the originally proposed subject for research. Such factors necessitate a review of the original research plan and suitable modifications to make the work more realistic and meaningful.

Describing the research process succinctly, Selltiz, Jahoda, Deutsch and Cook state that it consists of a number of closely related activities that overlap rather than following a strictly prescribed sequence. So interdependent are these activities that the first step of the research project largely determines the nature of the last. If subsequent procedures have not been taken into account in the early stages, serious difficulties may arise and prevent the completion of a study. Frequently these difficulties cannot be remedied at the time they become apparent because they are rooted in the earlier procedures. They can be avoided only by keeping in mind, at each step of the research process, the requirement of subsequent steps. To be sure, as research proceeds from the conception of a theme for a study through the gathering of data, to the production of a report, and the applications of the findings, the focus of attention will necessarily shift from one activity to the next. This shift reflects a difference in emphasis, however, rather than an exclusive concentration on one step. A mechanically consecutive sequence of procedures, in which one research step is entirely completed before the next is begun, is rarely, if ever, the experience of social scientists.[1]

We find that the research process consists of several important steps which are highly interdependent and each one of them determines significantly the nature of the other, and by the time the research project is complete each step in the process would have made its contribution to the final research. They may even overlap during the course of a project.

If any subsequent procedure has not been taken care of in the planning process, some serious kind of difficulties may arise in the course of research. Each step of the research process creates the requirements of the subsequent steps. For example, research begins from raising the problem to the gathering of the data, and from gathering of the data to their analysis and interpretation, finally to the writing of the report. As a project progresses from formulation of the problem through the collection of data to the drawing of conclusions, the focus of the researcher's attention necessarily shifts from one kind of activity to the other. These shifts reflect the differing emphasis at different points. Since all such processes are interdependent and each process reflects a difference in emphasis, it needs a separate treatment. But at the same time the researcher has to be constantly anticipating at each step in the research process, the requirements of the subsequent steps.[2]

Currently it is found that researchers and academicians seem to be overly concerned about the importance of research methods. Thus the objective of the research is to provide a study and then solve the problem that is raised. According to Emory and Cooper,

> Writers usually treat the research task as a sequential process involving a number of clearly defined steps. Variations are suggested for different situations but there is much similarity among sequences proposed. No one, however, claims that research is truly linear, completing each step before going to the next. Recycling circumventions, and skips tend to occur. Some steps are begun out of sequence, some are carried out simultaneously, and some may be omitted. In spite of these variations, the concept of sequence is useful, when we try to develop a project and keep it orderly as it unfolds. In this way the research process is one where the problem, its origin, selection, statement, exploration, and refinement is the predominant activity in the sequence.[3]

A research investigation may focus on a specific practical problem or may be concerned with more basic (pure) research issues, or a combination of these two alternatives. Although a particular investigation may quite legitimately be concerned with only one or the other of these two aspects, for the overall balanced development of scientific knowledge it is important that each of these two aspects are adequately represented in the collective research endeavour. Here, it is very important to note that availability of technique is an important factor in determining how research on any given study can be done. But persons skilled in given techniques are too often blinded by their special competencies. Their concern for technique dominates the decisions concerning the subject of study and how it will be studied. Some researchers think chiefly in terms of conducting surveys, some emphasize on the case study, while others seldom consider it. The creative researcher may benefit from this confusing array of options. The numerous combinations spawned by the abundance of tools may be used to construct alternative perspectives on the same problem. By creating a design using diverse methodologies, researchers are able to achieve greater insight than if they followed the most frequent method encountered in the literature or suggested by a disciplinary bias.[4]

The most common pattern for written research studies is based on the following major steps, which serve as guidelines for the research process:

(a) Articulating the purpose of research and formulating the problem.
(b) Selecting and developing an appropriate research design.
(c) Selection of methods for the collection of data and the nature and size of the sample.
(d) Statement of hypothesis.
(e) Collection of relevant data from the primary and secondary sources.
(f) Literature survey of existing relevant studies and writings.
(g) Tabulation and analysis of the data through suitable statistical methods keeping in view the objectives and hypotheses.
(h) Interpretation of data leading to findings and insights, through testing of the hypotheses.
(i) Critical analysis of the results.
(j) Presentation of the findings, discussion of the limitations of the study, and scope for further study.
(k) Preparation, editing and presentation of the report in an effective format to highlight the results of the study.

As stated earlier, these steps are not necessarily sequential and may have to be followed iteratively and simultaneously.

Similarly, each of the above-mentioned steps has its own relevance and significance which needs to be examined in detail. These will be discussed in the following chapters.

NOTES

1. C. Selltiz, M. Jahoda, M. Deutsch and S.W. Cook, *Research Methods in Social Relations*, Holt, Rinehart and Winston Inc., USA, 1961, p. 8.
2. B.C. Tandon, *Research Methodology in Social Sciences*, Chaitanya Publishing House, Allahabad, 1987, p. 68.
3. C.W. Emory and D.R. Cooper, *Business Research Methods*, Richard D. Irwin, Homewood, Illinois, 1991, pp. 71, 73.
4. Ibid., pp. 75, 82.

CHAPTER 3

Motivation for Research

An extremely important factor in pursuing and completing a research project, and in determining its quality is the presence of a highly motivated research scholar. Unlike other activities in the field of education such as teaching, training for development of skills for performance, laboratory experiments and preparation for examinations, which have more tangible and relatively early results, research activity is less structured and has great uncertainty associated with its results. Consequently, research activity is low in the list of priorities of teachers, students and institutions, and in the process is marginalized.

This may also explain why many scholars and teachers who register for doctoral research take an inordinately long time to complete their work, and sometimes give up their research work altogether. Hardly any effort is directed towards undertaking meaningful research as compared to the routine work of teaching and training, etc. However, it has been noticed that some individuals are highly motivated and pursue and complete research projects of good quality, in spite of all odds against them.

Similarly, some institutions give a very high priority to research and create conditions and incentives which encourage teachers, scholars and students to pursue research projects vigorously and contribute to the advancement of knowledge. It is, therefore, important to analyse and understand the factors and the process of motivation that lead to productive research.

In order to understand the process of motivation it would be relevant to examine some of the well known theories and concepts on the subject from the field of psychology and other behavioural sciences. This may be helpful in analysing the factors leading to high levels of motivation for research in individuals. While defining motivation, Terry and Franklin provide the viewpoints of various authors on the subject[1]:

- Motivation is a predisposition to act in a specific goal-directed manner. (Hellriegal and Slocum)
- Motivation may be defined as the state of an individual's perspective which represents the strength of his or her propensity to exert effort toward some particular behaviour. (Gibson)
- The term motivation refers to goal-directed behaviour. Goal-directed behaviour is characterized by the process of selecting and directing certain actions among voluntary activities to achieve goals. (Chung)
- Motives are expressions of a person's needs: hence they are personal and internal. (Davis)
- Motivation refers to expenditure of efforts toward a goal. (Dubrin)

These definitions have several common denominators to help us characterize the phenomenon of motivation:

1. An internal need energizes and activates human behaviour.
2. Drive is the inner force that propels behaviour in a specific direction.
3. Goals are the incentives or payoffs that reinforce private satisfaction.

Based on these concepts we can define motivation as follows: Motivation is the need or drive within an individual that drives him/her towards goal-oriented action. The extent of drive depends on the perceived level of satisfaction that can be achieved by the goal.

The term 'motive' is derived from the Latin word 'movere' which means, 'to move'. This property is common to all types of motives: they move the organism. The view that motivation is a key determinant of a person's behaviour is not a new one. In dealing with people and attempting to understand them, we give high priority to information concerning their motives.[2] According to Zimbardo,

> Motivation is a general term used to describe the process of starting, directing and maintaining physical and psychological activities. It is a broad concept that embraces such internal mechanisms as (a) preference for one activity over another, (b) enthusiasm and vigour of

a person's responses, and (c) persistence of organized patterns of action towards relevant goals. All behaviours are in some way motivated. People have reasons for doing what they do or for behaving in the manner that they do. Thus, human behaviour is directed towards certain goals and objectives. Such goal-directed behaviours revolve around the desire for need satisfaction. A need is a physiological, psychological or sociological want or desire that can be satisfied by reaching a desired goal.[3]

He further states that an unsatisfied need, drive, desire, or motive causes tension within the individual, leading him to engage in some kind of behaviour (to seek a means) to satisfy the need and thereby reduce the tension. This activity is directed towards a goal; arrival at the goal satisfies the need. For example, a thirsty person needs water, is driven by thirst, and is motivated by a desire for water in order to satisfy the need. Depending on how well the goal is accomplished, the inner state is modified as shown by the feedback loop. Thus, motivation begins with an unsatisfied inner state condition and ends with movement to release that unsatisfied condition, with goal-directed behaviour as a part of the process.[4]

In the opinion of Arnold, Robertson and Cooper, motivation involves factors which either push or pull us to behave in certain ways. It is essentially made up of three components:

(a) Direction, i.e. what a person is trying to do.
(b) Effort, i.e. how hard a person is trying.
(c) Persistence, i.e. how long a person continues trying.

It would be useful to highlight the key features of motivation:

1. People are usually motivated to do something. Some folks try hard and long to avoid work—that is motivated behaviour! Hence we should always remember the 'direction' component. What motivation usually means in the work context is motivation to tackle specified work duties.
2. It is easy to make the mistake of thinking that motivation is the only important determinant of work performance. What about ability? And, where a group is working together, what about coordination among the activities of group members?
3. Research on motivation occasionally uses persistence as

the outcome of interest. More often it uses effort, and performance. But performance depends on other factors too.[5]

In order to analyse the reasons why individuals are motivated towards research, first let us examine some of the well known theories and concepts relating to motivation. As explained above, motivation refers to inner drives and human needs that lead to particular kinds of thoughts, feelings and behaviour. Although there are many other psychological and social factors that affect human behaviour, such as attitudes, values, group norms, expectations, social conditioning, and culture, yet the mainsprings of human activity are the inner motives or needs. Motivation is, therefore, a highly significant aspect of human psychology and has been studied in great depth by psychologists.

In its simplest form, motivation may be described as motive-in-action. The term 'motive' here means a specific human need, and does not have any moral connotations—commonly attributed to the term 'motive' in colloquial speech, which refers to intention underlying an action. There are many well known theories of motivation, but among the most popular and easily understood theories is Abraham Maslow's theory of the Hierarchy of Needs.[6] It classifies human needs broadly into primary and secondary needs, which are further subdivided as follows:

Primary Needs

Physiological Needs (like hunger, thirst, survival, etc.)
Safety Needs (need for safety to human body, and security against natural and social dangers.)

Secondary Needs

Belongingness/Social Needs (need for belonging, love, acceptance, social relationships and social interactions, companionship and friendship, etc.)
Esteem Needs (these are of two types: first, which are internally oriented, like self-worth, confidence, competence, etc.; second, which are externally oriented like, need for status, recognition, appreciation, power and influence over others.)

Self-Actualization

(self fulfilment, personal growth, development of potential, etc. This refers to the human aspirations and persistent drive to achieve one's long-term goals, and to actualize one's full potential by becoming the kind of person one dreams about himself/herself in an ideal form).

Maslow in his theory, Hierarchy of Needs propounds that the above stated human needs can be arranged in a hierarchical order, i.e. the physiological and safety needs of human beings are more basic, hence they take priority over the secondary needs in determining human activity. From this point of view, the need hierarchy can be illustrated as a pyramid as shown in Fig. 3.1.

Maslow's theory also proposes that once the lower order or primary needs are reasonably satisfied, the dormant secondary needs get activated. Thus, allegorically, it may be said that man lives by bread alone when he has no bread; and man does not live by bread alone when he has bread.

Human needs follow some predictable patterns. When a need is activated, because of any psychological, social or physical stimulus or disequilibrium, a person strives for its satisfaction. If the need is not satisfied, it leads to frustration or other behaviours to cope with blockage in need satisfaction. When a

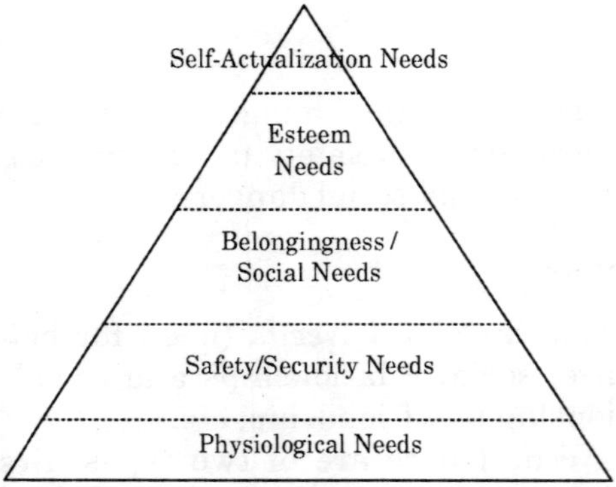

Fig. 3.1: Maslow's Hierarchy of Needs

Source: Adapted from Abraham H. Maslow, 'A Theory of Human Motivation', *Psychological Review*, Vol. 30, 1943, pp. 370-96.

need is satisfied, it ceases to be a motivator and becomes dormant until it is activated again.

There are other important theories which may also be helpful in understanding the phenomenon of motivation, especially for pursuing and engaging in productive and creative research. In this connection we shall briefly examine David McClelland's work on Achievement Motivation, and other related concepts.[7] Specifically examining the secondary motives, such as achievement, affiliation, and power needs, McClelland identifies the behaviour patterns and socialization process of persons with a strong need for achievement. Such individuals are highly competitive with high standards of achievement, want quick feedback on their performance, tend to take calculated risks, like to innovate and improve upon existing conditions, and wish to excel in all their pursuits. The need for achievement may have some relevance in motivating individuals to pursue challenging research work. On the basis of these theories of motivation, we can attempt to explain the possible causes of high or low motivation for pursuing research among students, teachers and scholars.

It can be inferred from the above theories that if research is pursued as a means of earning a livelihood to meet the basic needs of an individual, it is unlikely to be a creative or inspiring work, and the commitment of the researcher may be quite low. On the other hand, if a person pursues research as a means of satisfying higher order needs, like need for recognition, self-worth, professional status, achievement or self-actualization, it may lead to a higher level of commitment, productivity and creativity.

Another concept which may be relevant in this context is the relationship between the probability of success and level of motivation. Studies have revealed an inverted U type relationship between these two variables, i.e. a very high or a very low probability of success reduce the level of motivation, while a 50 per cent or thereabouts range of probability of success lead to high motivation, as shown in Fig. 3.2.

The probability of success usually being low in research, it is likely that the motivation for research may not be as high as in other academic activities with a moderate probability of success.

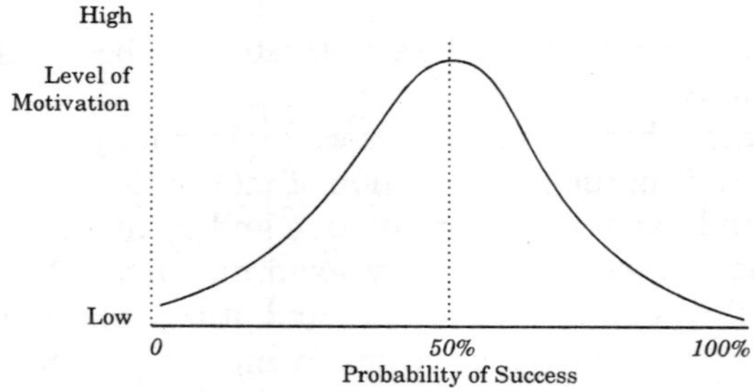

Fig. 3.2: Relationship between Probability of Success and Level of Motivation

To apply the theories of motivation, the distinction and relationship between 'motives' and 'incentives' should be understood. While motives refer to underlying latent needs, incentives refer to perceived rewards, satisfactions, or gains by achievement of a goal that one may get as a result of a particular activity. The incentives, therefore, play a key role in activating the latent motives to pursue certain goals and activities. Therefore, if incentives and rewards for research are much lower than other activities, a person may be relatively more motivated towards other activities than research. In other words, if research is a low paid, low social status, and unrecognized activity, and the psychological, social and material incentives associated with it are of a low order, then in all likelihood research activity may be marginalized.

The psychological concept that appears to be relevant here is the 'approach' and 'avoidance' behaviour based on hope of success or fear of failure in a given activity. An individual's tendency to avoid work, which is considered important, may be on account of a subconscious fear of failure or perceived low probability of success. Research, being a complex and ambiguous activity, with uncertain results, may often arouse fear of failure, anxiety and avoidance behaviour, and consequent delays in the completion of research work. As we know, unlike other academic activities, there is usually a long time gap between one's efforts and results in research work. This may also lead to frustration and low levels of motivation for research among students and teachers.

The research supervisors and guides can play a significant

role in sustaining high levels of motivation for research in individuals by providing a supportive relationship; clearly defining objectives, scope, topic and hypotheses for research; and imparting a sense of purpose. They can provide valuable guidance in the search for relevant literature, sources of data collection, positive reinforcement for progress of research work, help in identifying specific stages and 'milestones' for research, progression and enabling the researcher to experience success in reaching such 'milestones'.

At the institutional level, it is extremely important to give a high priority to research through tangible measures like resource allocation and creation of an institutional framework for recognizing and rewarding high quality research work. Further, it is essential to integrate such incentives with career growth and academic status. Only when such conditions are created in institutions, and individuals with high motivation for original research are offered the opportunity, support and incentives to pursue research, can we expect academic institutions to produce high quality research for the advancement of knowledge and betterment of standards in education in different fields of study.

In the field of performing arts like music, research is usually given low priority unlike the fields of science, technology, and medicine. Most often the emphasis is an performance skills rather than on advancement of knowledge and creativity through research in the performing arts. But we need to highlight the fact that if a performing art is devoid of research-based knowledge and creativity, it may degenerate into a vocation, and may not develop to higher levels of scientific and aesthetic excellence. Perhaps this may explain why many vibrant, rich and valuable traditions of performing arts have withered away, and are at best only mentioned in historical narratives of the glorious past.

NOTES

1. G.R. Terry and S.G. Franklin, *Principles of Management*, A.I.T.B.S., New Delhi, 1997, p. 298.
2. D.M. Pestonjee, *Motivation and Job Satisfaction*, Macmillan, New Delhi, 1991, p. 3.
3. J.M. Ivancevich, J.H. Donnelly, Jr. and J.L. Gibson, *Management Principles and Functions*, Richard D. Irwin, Inc., USA, 1998, p. 368.

4. Ibid., pp. 368-9.
5. J. Arnold, I.T. Robertson and C.L. Cooper, *Work Psychology*, Macmillan, 1995, p. 173.
6. Abraham H. Maslow, *Motivation and Personality*, Harper and Row, New York, 1995, pp. 93-8.
7. D.C. McClelland, *The Achieving Society*, Van Nostrand, Princeton, N.J., 1961.

CHAPTER 4

Research Design

To initiate any research study, it is essential to develop a suitable research design specifying the method, characteristics and scope for the collection, measurement and analysis of data. The research design is dependent on the objectives of a research project, based on the formulation of the research problem. And helps in specifying the types of information needed, and the procedures that may be necessary to obtain and analyse the relevant information in the most economical and efficient manner. The following definitions by leading authors on the subject will help us in understanding the essential elements of research design:

The research design is the plan and structure of investigation so conceived as to obtain answers to research questions. The plan is the overall scheme or programme of the research. It includes an outline of what the investigator will do from writing hypotheses and their operational implications to the final analysis of data. A structure is the framework, organisation or configuration of . . . the relations among variables of a study. A research design expresses both the structure of the research problem and the plan of investigation used to obtain empirical evidence on relations of the problem.[1]

A research design is the arrangement of conditions for collection and analysis of data in a manner that aims to combine relevance to the research purpose with economy in procedure. Once the research problem has been formulated clearly enough to specify the types of information needed, the investigator must work out his research design.[2]

The research design constitutes the blueprint for the collection, measurement, and analysis of data. It aids the scientist in the allocation of his limited resources by posing crucial choices: Is the blueprint to include experiments, interviews, observation, the analysis of records, simulation, or combination of these? Are the methods of data collection and the research situation to be highly structured? Is an intensive study of a large sample necessary? Should the analysis be primarily quantitative or qualitative?[3]

The above definitions present different facets of research design. However, we can identify the elements of a good research design from the following definitions by Emory and Cooper:

> First, the design is a plan for selecting the sources and types of information relevant to the research question. Second, it is a framework for specifying the relationships among the study's variables. Third, it is a blueprint for outlining all of the procedures from the hypothesis to the analysis of data. The design provides for answers to such questions as: What techniques will be used? How will time and cost constraints be dealt with?[4]

Commenting on research design Wilkinson and Bhandarkar state that designing, by forewarning us of future difficulties ensures against wasteful expenditure of money, time and energy. It could be described as the process making decisions by anticipating the situation in which the decision has to be carried out. It is thus a process of deliberate anticipation directed towards bringing an expected situation under control. The research designer understandably cannot hold all decisions in his/her head. Even if that was possible it would be difficult to understand their interrelationship. Therefore, decisions are recorded by using relevant symbols or concepts. Such a symbolic construction may be called the research design or model. The model makes overall evaluation of the total plan. It is on this basis that the researcher can see the whole study structure and also realize the place and importance of the successive steps that he/she will be required to take in the total scheme.[5]

The blueprint of the research design emerges from some basic decisions regarding the key elements in a sequential order. Significant decisions need to be made in the following aspects of research:

1. Specific research problem as formulated by the researcher and the nature and quantum of data required.
2. Rationale of the study.
3. Sources from where data can be obtained.
4. Scope of the study in terms of time period and the regions or sectors to be covered.
5. Size of the sample or the number of cases to be examined.

6. The basis for sample selection and the type of sample to be chosen.
7. Methods and techniques to be adopted for data collection.
8. Method and approach for analysing data.
9. Identification of solutions to the above stated issues keeping in mind the constraints of resources, time and skills available to achieve the objectives of research in the most efficient possible manner.

In short, research design is a strategy which specifies the methods and procedures for the collection, measurement and analysis of data. Unfortunately, there is no simple classification of research designs which covers the variations found in practice. The following are some of the major types of studies.

Exploratory or Formulative Studies

Exploratory research is appropriate for studies in subject areas where the developed data are limited. In most studies exploration is the first stage of a project and is used to orient the researcher and the study. The objective of exploration is the development of hypotheses and not to test them.

Many exploratory studies are conducted for the purpose of formulating a problem either for a more precise investigation or developing a hypothesis. An exploratory study may however have other functions:

1. Increasing the investigator's familiarity with the phenomena he wishes to investigate in a subsequent, more highly structured, study, or with the setting in which he plans to carry out such a study.
2. Clarifying concepts.
3. Establishing priorities for further research.
4. Gathering information about practical possibilities for carrying out research in real life settings.
5. Providing a census of problems regarded as urgent by people working in a given field.

For whatever purpose an exploratory study is undertaken, ingenuity and good luck will inevitably play a part in determining its productiveness. Nevertheless, it is possible to suggest certain methods that are likely to be specially fruitful in the search for important variables and meaningful hypotheses. These methods include:

(a) A review of the related pertinent literature.
(b) A survey of people who have had practical experience with the problem to be studied.
(c) An analysis of 'insight stimulating' examples.

Most exploratory studies utilize one or more of these approaches.[6]

Literature Search: The first step in an exploratory study is to do a survey of literature in the relevant subject area. One of the simplest ways of economizing on effort in an enquiry is to review and build upon the work already done by others. In a study of the type that we are discussing here, the focus of review is on hypotheses that may serve as leads for further investigation. Hypotheses may have been explicitly stated by the previous workers, the task then is to gather the various hypotheses that have been put forward, to evaluate their usefulness as the basis for further research, and to consider whether they suggest new hypotheses. More frequently, however, an exploratory study is concerned with an area in which hypotheses have not yet been formulated. The task then is to review the available material with sensitivity to the hypotheses that may be derived from it.[7]

Studying the secondary sources of information is the simplest and quickest, and perhaps the most economical way of finding hypotheses. A research scholar can scan, in a short period of time, a large volume of published literature and gather ideas from it. The most useful sources of available literature on a subject include books, journals and periodicals, newspapers, recorded documents, etc. In addition, special catalogues and subject guides available in libraries can be helpful in this search. Doctoral theses and M.Phil. dissertations contain valuable information on various specialized topics. A literature search can provide an excellent background on the areas of interest and supply a number of good leads if one has a creative mind.

Survey of Experienced Persons: This involves interviewing such specialists and experts who have acquired, in the routine of their work, a reservoir of experience that could be of great help and value to the researcher. The purpose of the experience survey is to gather and synthesise such experience. The most important problem in this case is that of selecting respondents. It is important to select people so as to ensure a representation of different types of experiences. For interviewing these experienced individuals it would be necessary for a researcher to be familiar with the important issues and questions in the area of research.

Commenting on the subject Selltiz, Jahoda and others write:

> In an experience survey it is a waste of time and effort to interview people who have little competence or little relevant experiences, or who lack ability to communicate their experience. An individual may have worked in a field for a number of years and not necessarily be a good informant. Perhaps the most direct method of selecting informants is to ask strategically placed administrators working in the area one desires to study to point out the most informative, experienced and analytical people. Although this does not guarantee insight stimulating respondents, one does obtain through this method people with a reputation for good experience and good ideas.
>
> Before any systematic attempt is made to collect the insights of experienced practitioners it is, of course, necessary to have some preliminary ideas of the important issues in the area. One source of such ideas is a bibliographical survey. Even in more systematic interviewing of later informants, it is essential to maintain a considerable degree of flexibility. The purpose of providing the interview with structure is to ensure that all people interviewed respond to the questions the researcher wishes to have answered; however, the formulative and discovery functions of the experience survey require that the interviews always allowed the respondent to raise issues and questions the investigator has not previously considered.[8]

Insight Stimulating Examples: Remarkable theoretical insights have been stimulated by intensive and holistic studies by a few renowned researchers and scientists of some specific phenomenon. This type of approach has been described as 'insight stimulating experience'. This is particularly useful as an exploratory approach in relatively unformulated areas, where there is little experience or information available to serve as a guide. In this method the emphasis is on understanding the subject of investigation as a whole and all aspects of the case are intensively investigated.

Such a study may focus on a particular phenomenon in a given time or region and may be specifically based on individuals, situations, groups or communities. The method of study may be a detailed examination of existing records, manuscripts, instruments, and may also be based on unstructured interviews or participant observation or some other relevant method of data collection.

The exploratory research approaches may be particularly suitable in the field of music and other performing arts.

Descriptive Studies

Research based on the descriptive method may be called descriptive studies, which are characterized by fact finding with adequate interpretation. The objective in a descriptive study is to learn the who, what, when, where and how of a topic. The study may be simple or complex, and may be done in many settings. The simplest descriptive study concerns a univariate question or hypothesis in which we ask about, or state something about the size, form, distribution or existence of a variable.[9]

Descriptive studies can utilize a wide range of methods in data collection and analysis and need not be limited to any one method. Some of the methods commonly used in such studies include: the survey method; continuity description; case study method; activity analysis; and library and documentary search.

Although such studies use a wide range of techniques, they may not have the flexibility of the exploratory studies. The procedures used in a descriptive study must be carefully planned. Because the aim is to obtain complete and accurate information, the research design must make greater provision for protection against bias than is required in exploratory studies. In such studies the research questions presuppose much prior knowledge of the problem to be investigated as contrasted with the questions that form the basis for exploratory studies. The investigator must be able to define what it is that he/she wants to measure and must find adequate methods for measuring it. In collecting evidence for a study of this sort, what is needed is not so much flexibility as a clear formulation of what and who is to be measured and techniques for valid and reliable measurements.[10]

Causal Studies

In contrast to the descriptive or exploratory studies, which are primarily concerned with investigating the existing factual position of a phenomenon, the causal studies are aimed at discovering causal relationships between two or more sets of variables. It is often desirable to follow a two-step procedure for causal studies, especially when the direction of a research project is not clear. In such a situation the first stage can be largely exploratory, aimed at formulating hypotheses and developing the specific research design. The second stage can be elevated to collection of data and testing of the hypotheses for the causal study. Causal studies seek to determine the effect that a variable(s) has on another (or others) or why certain outcomes are obtained. The concept of causality is grounded in the logic of hypothesis testing which in turn produces inductive conclusions. Such conclusions are probabilistic and thus can never be demonstrated with certainty.[11]

There are various possibilities and methods of studying causal relationships between variables. The *Causal Comparative Method* is utilized for discovering possible causes for the phenomenon being examined by comparing subjects in which a characteristic is present with similar subjects in which it is absent or present to a lesser degree. This method can be utilized only to explore causal relationships, but cannot give a definitive confirmation of the same.

Another form is the correlational study, in which the purpose is to explore the relationships between two sets of data through the use of correlation coefficients. Through this method the magnitude of relationship between two variables can be measured, but it cannot determine the cause and effect relationship between the two or whether a third variable is influencing both the variables.

Compared to these two methods the *Experimental Research* design, if used with proper controls, is more dependable for examining causal relationships. In this method the treatment variable is manipulated and its effects on the dependent variable are examined in a particular group called the experimental group. The other group, which has similar characteristics as the experimental group, is not subjected to such treatment and is considered to be the 'control group'. The observations of the relationship between the changes in the treatment variable and the outcomes as recorded in the experimental group are compared to the control group, which lead to inferences for research findings. The experimental method is considered relatively more effective for testing "theories" about causal relationships. However, it is widely accepted that the complexity of relationship between variables is not easy to discover, especially in the field of social sciences and arts, because of the complexity and subjectivity in the researches involving human beings.

While summing up the essential elements of research design Emory and Cooper conclude that it is the strategy for a study as well as the plan by which the strategy is to be carried out. It specifies the methods and procedures for the collection, measurement, and analysis of data. Unfortunately, there is no simple classification of research designs which covers the variations found in practice. Some of the major perspectives on designs are : (1) Exploratory versus formalized, (2) Observational versus survey, (3) Experimental versus ex post facto, (4) Descriptive versus causal, (5) Cross-Sectional versus longitudinal, (6) Case versus statistical, and (7) Field versus laboratory versus simulation.[12]

NOTES

1. Fred N. Kerlinger, *Foundations of Behavioural Research*, Holt, Rinehart and Winston Inc., USA, 1986, p. 279.
2. C. Selltiz, M. Jahoda, M. Deutsch and S.W. Cook, *Research Methods in Social Relations*, Holt, Rinehart and Winston Inc., USA, 1961, p. 50.
3. Bernard S. Philips, *Social Research Strategy and Tactics*, Macmillan, New York, 1971, p. 93.
4. C.W. Emory, and D.R. Cooper, *Business Research Methods*, Richard D. Irwin, Homewood, Illinois, 1991, p. 139.
5. T.S. Wilkinson, and P.L. Bhandarkar, *Methodology and Techniques of Social Research*, Himalaya Publishing House, Bombay, 1979, pp. 86-7.
6. Selltiz et al., op. cit., pp. 51, 53.

7. Ibid., p. 53
8. Ibid., p. 51
9. C.W. Emory and D.R. Cooper, op. cit., p. 148.
10. Selltiz et al., op. cit., pp. 66-7.
11. Emory and Cooper, op. cit., p. 161.
12. Ibid., p. 161.

CHAPTER 5

Selection and Formulation of Research Topic

The process of research consists of various steps and if any of the necessary procedures has not been followed in the planning process, the researcher may have to face some serious difficulties. This may arise in the course of research that may even obstruct the completion of the study. The research process includes the following steps: Selection and formulation of the problem, designing the study, data collection, analysis, and interpretations and conclusions of findings.

SELECTION OF RESEARCH PROBLEM

The topic of study may be selected by an individual researcher having intellectual interests or by an institution. Institutions generally tend to select topics involving specific problems or particular situations. On the other hand, a researcher because of intellectual curiosity may be interested in exploring some general subject matter about which relatively little is known, or may select subjects that have already been studied to some extent. The researcher may also be interested in a phenomenon or field that has a highly developed theoretical system, but needs re-testing of the old theory on the basis of new facts. Scientific and intellectual interests of researchers may suggest an equally wide range of topics for research. Such interests are likely to lead to general questions, and to a concern with specific situations as examples of general classes of phenomena rather than as objects of interest in their own right. As mentioned earlier the researcher with intellectual curiosity may be interested in phenomenon that have already been studied to some extent. In such matters a new study may be done specifying more exactly the conditions under which a given phenomenon appears and how it may be affected by other factors.[1]

One of the recurring problems in the Indian education system is that a student may complete the postgraduate course with a brilliant first class depending solely on half-a-dozen textbooks, but he/she may be incapable of identifying a research problem. It is commonly observed that when a student with a Master's degree turns to research, there is a sudden discontinuity in the academic process which puts him/her in a difficult situation. The only remedy to this problem is developing a sense of curiosity among students which would nudge them towards collecting material on subjects of their interest, processing it, drawing conclusions, and putting them to test. This sort of exercise can considerably enhance the capacity of students to undertake research.

It has been suggested that students working toward a higher degree, should arrive on campus with a list of problems isolated from their recent professional experience. And out of which they should select tentatively one problem that is most crucial and feasible for their thesis work. The faculty would then evaluate their selection. But considerable differences are found in this initiative which encourages independence in students. And these are caused by variations in the native intelligence of students, types of academic courses pursued, and kinds of previous professional experience. In some cases, of course, there has been no educational experience, as students have proceeded to do their doctoral programmes directly after completing the Bachelor's and Master's degrees. Further, student participation in larger studies, in which the faculty adviser is interested, is desirable and can often be arranged.[2]

Another important factor in the selection of the subject of research is the fact whether the research problem has been identified by the researcher or suggested by the supervisor. On this issue rigid rules cannot be laid down in general terms, except that both the supervisor and the candidate should have a sustainable interest in the subject of research and it should be acceptable to both of them. The imposition of a research topic by the supervisor and its total acceptance by the candidate may destroy the elements of spontaneity and authenticity, which are essential for a good quality research study. The supervisor can at best suggest a broad area of research, from which selection of a specific research problem should be the responsibility of the one who actually does the research.

An equally important factor in selecting a research topic is an individual's value judgement. More often than not personal preference determines the selection of the research topic which depends on value judgement. Besides, social conditions under which research is conducted influence the preferences of institutions or individuals in the selection of the topic. It is possible that if a subject is given importance in the society, it would get preference over other subjects. Though personal values inevitably influence the choice of topics, it would be incorrect to assume that personal values are the only determinant in selecting a topic for research. There are other factors which play a more important role. Sometimes social interest, need for comparative study, and socio-economic environment determine the values which influence the choice of a research study.

The following are some valuable suggestions by J.C. Almack on how to select a research problem:

1. Analyse what is known, including the historical record.
2. Look for gaps or deficiencies in explanations—that is, for 'areas of darkness'.
3. Watch for incongruities and contradictions, the points of controversy, the untested conclusions.
4. Follow clues and suggestions obtained from reading, conferences, and thinking. Observe where activity is the greatest and where there is evidence of neglect. Keep a memorandum of ideas, hypotheses and problems as they occur.[3]

W.A. McCall of Teachers' College of Columbia University suggests five ways to identify research problems:

1. To become a scholar in one or more specialities as early as possible.
2. To read, listen and work critically, reflectively.
3. To consider every obstacle an opportunity for the exercise of ingenuity instead of an insuperable barrier.
4. To start a research and watch problems bud out of it.
5. To keep in view the problems already found.[4]

The following suggestions in the selection of research problems have been vividly expressed by N.J. Salkind:[5]

1. The selection of problem you want to work on is terribly important for two reasons. First, research takes a great deal of time and energy as you want to be sure that the problem you select interests you. You will work so hard throughout this project, that continuing to work on it, even if it is the most interesting project, may at times become too much. Just think of what it would be like if you were not interested! Second, the problem you select is only the first step in the research process. If this goes well the remaining steps which are no less important, have a good chance of going well also. So it is advised that the researcher must select a problem that he is genuinely interested in.
2. Mostly the enthusiasm of the researchers is encouraged by their professors or supervisors and they consider it an essential quality. Enthusiasm is not incompatible with being objective and dispassionate about the actual research process (not the content). Sometimes, and this is especially true for beginning research students, researchers see their question as one of such magnitude and importance that they fail to listen to those around them, including their adviser, who are trying to help them formulate their problem in such a way as to make it precise, and in the long run easier to address. The researcher should be committed to his ideas and really like his topic a lot but not so much that it clouds his judgement as to the practical and right way to do things. At the same time it is not wise to stick to the first idea which comes to mind. Because second and third ideas are usually much more refined, easier to do, and more manageable than the first one.
3. The researcher should be realistic and attempt only what he can finish, given other demands on his time and energy. If he finds what has been done by reading previous studies and use that information as a foundation, he will surely come up with a research problem of significance and value. There is a fine line

between what has been done and what is important to do next, based on what has been done. Part of his job is to learn how to build and elaborate on the results of previous research without duplicating previous efforts.

4. One should not disregard personal experience as an important source of ideas. In some relatively rare cases, students know from the beginning what they want to select as a research area and what research questions they want to ask. But for many others there is more anxiety and doubt than confidence. Before beginning the all important literature review, one should first take a look at these suggestions for where he might find interesting questions that are well worth considering as research topics. His own experiences shape the type of person he is. So he should not ignore his past when considering the general area and content of a research question, even if he can not see an immediate link between these experiences and possible research activities. By continuous reading he may find ways that create that link.

According to C.R. Kothari, a researcher should keep the following points in mind while selecting a research problem or a subject for research:

1. A subject which is overdone should not be normally chosen, for it will be a difficult task to throw any new light in such a case.
2. A controversial subject should not become the choice of an average researcher.
3. Too narrow or too vague problems should be avoided.
4. The subject selected for research should be familiar and feasible so that the related research material or sources of research are within one's reach. Even then it is quite difficult to supply definitive ideas concerning how the researcher should obtain ideas for his research. For this purpose, a researcher should contact an expert or a professor in the university who is already engaged in research. He may as well read articles published in current literature available on the subject and may think how the techniques and ideas discussed therein might

be applied to the solution of other problems. He may discuss with others what he has in mind concerning a problem. In this way we should make all possible efforts in selecting a problem.

5. The importance of the subject, the qualifications and the training of a researcher, the costs involved, the time factor are few other criteria that must also be considered in selecting a problem. In other words, before the final selection of a problem is done, a researcher must ask himself the following questions:
   (a) Whether he is well equipped in terms of his background to carry out the research?
   (b) Whether the study falls within the budget he can afford?
   (c) Whether the necessary cooperation can be obtained from those who must participate in research as subjects?

   If the answers to all these questions are in the affirmative, one may become sure so far as the practicability of the study is concerned.
6. The selection of the problem must be preceded by a preliminary study. This may not be necessary when the problem requires the conduct of a research closely similar to one that has already been done. But when the field of inquiry is relatively new and does not have available a set of well developed techniques, a brief feasibility study must always be undertaken.[6]

The various approaches to identify a research problem have been aptly summed up by F.L. Whitney. He points out that the research problem originates from a situation of need, where unsolved difficulties appear. If this need is felt, the thinking process begins with recognition of a specific problem for study. Such activities as the following should be engaged in: analyse everything known already, all previous research; look for gaps in explanations; find untested conclusions; follow clues; recognize conflicts in experience; survey concrete suggestions for needed research; become a scholar in one or more specialities; read, listen and work continuously and reflectively; consider obstacles as challenges for ingenuity; start a research and watch problems bud out of it; have a constant attitude of questioning every procedure in the field of interest; look for actual evidence on current procedures and estimate the reliability of knowledge available about important issues. The problem should be carefully analysed so that all of its implications may be definitely apparent. This will reveal its limitations and make efforts towards solution more effective.[7]

In the light of the above observations it can be summarized that the process of selecting a research problem requires careful consideration of various factors. It is worthwhile to examine these factors and anticipate their probable effects on the research activity and its outcomes, rather than to be bogged down with problems at various subsequent stages. The following factors should be kept in mind while selecting a research problem: (1) Practicability and feasibility; (2) Novelty and oiginality; (3) Contribution to the subject; (4) Data availability; (5) Time and resources; and (6) Utility and applicability.

After identifying the broad area in which one would like to do research, the researcher must have two considerations in mind: personal interest and competence. To do sustained work on a given problem and to put one's intellectual efforts fully into it, could turn out to be uninteresting and meaningless unless one has a genuine interest in the problem. At the same time interest and inclination must be matched by competence before deciding the area of research. And competence can be developed and cultivated by learning new techniques in the field of research methodology.

Formulation of a Research Problem

Albert Einstein and L. Infield have rightly emphasized that the formulation of a problem is often more essential than its solution. The selection of a topic for research does not immediately equip the investigator to consider the kind of data to collect, the methods to be used and how to analyse the data. Before planning these steps a scientific formulation of a problem is not as simple as it may appear. Darcony has aptly stated: 'Looking back, I think, it was more difficult to see what the problems were than to solve them.' This is particularly true in the field of music and fine arts, where the phenomena are not as easily measurable and definable as in the realm of science. Being creative arts, these disciplines are more amenable to exploration and innovation as an expression rather than a subject of organized and systematic investigation. However, the historical, comparative, literature survey and analytical approaches of search can be fruitfully conducted to preserve the heritage and enrich the development of theory in such fields. This can be done as in other fields of humanities and social sciences, through careful collection, observation and study of empirical data. Systematic knowledge acquired by the researcher, training and personal talents, contribute towards sensitizing him/her to perceive a research problem.

On the formulation of a research problem Jahoda and others state that unfortunately it happens not infrequently that an investigator attempts to jump immediately from the selection of a topic to the collection of observations. At best, this means that the researcher will be faced with the task of formulating a problem after the data collection: at worst that he/she will not produce a scientific inquiry at all. Scientific inquiry is an undertaking geared to the solution of problems. The first step in the formulation of a research topic is to make the problem concrete and explicit.

Although the selection of a research topic may be determined by other than scientific considerations, the formulation of the topic into a research problem is the first step in a scientific inquiry and as such should be influenced primarily by the requirements of scientific procedure. However, there is no foolproof rule which can guide the investigator in formulating significant questions about a given research area. Here, the training and gifts of the individual are of major importance. As Cohen and Nagel (1934) point out: 'The ability to perceive in some brute experience the occasion for a problem, and especially a problem whose solution has a bearing on the solution of other problems, is not a common talent among men. . . . It is a mark of scientific genius to be sensitive to difficulties where less gifted people pass by untroubled by doubt.'

Yet it is possible to enumerate some conditions that experience has shown to be conducive to the formulation of a significant problem. Among these conditions are systematic immersion in the relevant subject matter through first-hand observation, the study of existing literature and discussions with persons who have accumulated much practical experience in the field of study. Important as these conditions are in the formulation of a research project, they contain a danger. In social science, as elsewhere, habits of thought may interfere with the discovery of the new and the unexpected unless preliminary first-hand observation, reading and discussions are conducted in a curious and imaginative frame of mind.[8]

In the formulation of a problem for research three principal components are to be followed:

1. Discovery of a Problem in Need of Solution: The scope of the problem should be such that the topic selected is of a manageable size: this is a necessary step in the initial stages of problem formulation. If the problem is too wide and unmanageable it may lead to the failure of the project. But at the same time if the problem is too small, it may not be a real challenge to the researcher and there is a possibility of his losing interest in due course. The researcher must immerse himself thoroughly in the area of the subject matter within which he is supposed to pose a specific problem. The researcher should also be well equipped to confront the difficulties that may arise during the formulation of a problem. He/she should be well conversant with the relevant theories in the concerned area and the necessary available literature. Discussions and consultations with persons having rich practical experience in the relevant field of study can be very useful in the formulation of the problem.

2. Specification of the Question: The question which has originated the research must be specifically and clearly stated. A particular observation becomes necessary to answer a specific question. When the answers are found to these specific questions, it is possible to find a solution to the problem.

The initial phase in the process of problem formulation is to articulate the originating questions. Such questions identify the beginning of certain problems and challenges which need to be resolved through the research study. When these questions are formulated in specific terms in order to identify areas where answers to them can be searched for, they acquire the status of a research problem. There are two kinds of originating questions. One that requires the exploration and verification of a specific body of social facts; and the other focuses on the search for patterns and relationship between classes of social variables.

3. *The Rationale of Questions:* Rationale is the statement of reasons why a particular question is worth raising. The rationale of a question helps to distinguish between a valuable and trivial question. The conceptualization and understanding of the problem may be made clear by answering such questions. Thus, the questions may be of either theoretical interest or practical utility. It must not neglect either of these two.[9] We need to distinguish between two kinds of rationale, the practical and the theoretical. The former makes a case for a question by pointing out that its answers will be of practical value to people. And the latter makes a case for a question by showing that a question may be considered as one worth asking since its answer would enlarge the scope of its theory or conceptual framework or the proposition which is to be tested.

Literature Survey

It has been found from experience that research topics are sometimes finalized without an adequate literature survey of the research work that has already been done on the subject, and without carefully examining whether the chosen topic will yield useful results, fresh information and meaningful insights. To avoid such pitfalls in the selection process a systematic approach to literature survey is desirable for exploring the existing literature on the subject. This approach as illustrated in Fig. 5.1 proceeds from broad general references to very specific and specialized studies on the subject of research.

In short, it is advisable to carefully select a research topic which is narrow in scope, and in addition to sustaining the interest of the researcher also has the relevant material and necessary data for the study. The factors described above need to be kept in view, while formulating the problem, so that the findings of the research are useful in advancing knowledge and making a meaningful contribution to the chosen field.

State your idea and research subject in broad general terms by using general sources, Reference Books, General Magazines, Bibliographies, Newspapers, etc.

↓

Search the existing knowledge and information through related secondary sources on the subject (Articles/Books on the subject, Research Reviews, etc.)

↓

Search the primary sources on actual research already done on the subject (Specialized Journals, Scholarly Books, Research Abstracts of published and unpublished works)

↓

Organize the points and information as notes to focus on your topic

↓

Write your proposal giving specific topic of research and its rationale in the light of literature review

Fig. 5.1: Steps in Reviewing Literature for Writing a Research Proposal

NOTES

1. C. Selltiz, M. Jahoda, M. Deutsch and S.W. Cook, *Research Methods in Social Relations,* Holt, Rinehart and Winston, Inc., USA, 1961, p. 27.
2. F.L. Whitney, *The Elements of Research,* Prentice Hall, Inc., New York, 1954, pp. 70-1.
3. J.C. Almack, *Research and Thesis Writing,* Houghton Miffin Co., Boston, 1930, p. 48.
4. W.A. McCall, *How to Experiment in Education,* Macmillan, New York, pp. 7-8.
5. N.J. Salkind, *Exploring Research,* Prentice Hall, New Jersey, 1991, p. 53.
6. C.R. Kothari, *Research Methodology: Methods and Techniques,* Wiley Eastern Ltd., New Delhi, 1985, p. 37.
7. F.L. Whitney, loc. cit., p. 95.
8. Selltiz et al., loc. cit., pp. 30-1.
9. C.R. Reddy, *Research Methodology in Social Sciences,* Daya Publishing House, Delhi, 1987, p. 52.

CHAPTER 6

Hypothesis

One of the most important elements in empirical research is the formulation of perceptive and testable hypotheses. The hypothesis performs a pivotal role in conducting an empirical study: it crystallizes the research problem, as well as facilitates data collection and analysis. A good quality research, therefore, depends to a great extent on suitable formulation of hypotheses. According to the *Webster's Dictionary* a hypothesis is 'a proposition, condition or principle which is assumed, perhaps without belief, in order to draw out its logical consequences and by this method, to test its accord with facts which are known or may be determined'.[1] A hypothesis can also be defined as a conjectural statement positing the relations between two or more phenomena, usually referred to as a 'Cause and Effect'.[2]

Importance and Scope of Hypothesis

After the formulation of the research problem the most important step in research is formulating a hypothesis, because sometimes the final hypothesis, which fits all the evidence becomes the main conclusion inferred from the study. The word 'hypothesis' generally refers to a definite interpretation of a given set of facts, which is put forth as a tentative suggestion and remains partly or wholly unverified. Once it is established, it ceases to be a hypothesis and becomes a theory or explanatory principle.[3]

Discussing the importance of a hypothesis Cohen and Nagel emphasize that it would be impossible to take a single step forward in any inquiry unless we begin with a suggested explanation or solution of the problem which originated it. Such tentative explanations emerge from the subject matter of the study and the researcher's previous knowledge. When formulated as propositions, the explanations are called hypotheses.[4] Thus hypotheses guide the researcher through a bewildering jungle of facts to review and select only those that are relevant to the solution of the proposed problem. Collection of facts merely for the sake of collecting them will yield no fruits; to be fruitful, one should collect facts which provide the pros and cons of a point of view or proposition. Such a point of view or proposition is the hypothesis.[5]

Hypothesis is a tentative statement of perceived relationship between cause and effect or between two variables in a given phenomenon. For example, one may put forward as a hypothesis that the younger generation is more interested in western and pop music than in classical music, thus a relationship between age and aesthetic inclination is being predicted. To support or reject this hypothesis it would require empirical testing through data from a representative sample of population.

A hypothesis has often been described as the centre point of a research work from where one can look back at the research problem and look forward to data collection. Thus based upon known facts with the help of theoretical knowledge new facts are discovered. The deductions formulated in this process are known as hypotheses. Hypotheses state what we are looking for and after deriving certain conclusions, new hypotheses are formed. In other words, a hypothesis as it is based on facts and theory may be defined as a proposition or a condition which can be visualized. Its role is to suggest explanations for certain facts, to guide the investigation of others and to test their validity. Every theory permits the formulation of additional hypotheses. After the hypothesis is tested and found correct or incorrect, the theory is revised or reformulated. And this is the purpose of research.

Hypothesis provides a base and objective through which the researcher can rationalize statements systematically and relate logically known facts to intelligent guesses about unknown conditions. Besides, it can be very helpful in providing the basis for writing the conclusions of the research study and the research may test each hypothesis conveniently and may state the conclusions.

Types of Hypotheses

Though various kinds of hypotheses have been described by authors, there are three main types of hypotheses, namely: Descriptive, Relational and Causal Hypotheses.

A descriptive hypothesis is a proposition that typically states the existence, size, form or distribution of some variables. Such hypotheses encourage researchers to clarify their thinking about the likely relationships between variables and the implications of the hypotheses, being supported or rejected by the findings.

A relational hypothesis is a statement that describes a relationship between two variables pertaining to a particular case or phenomenon. In such hypotheses the relationship between two variables is not specified, which indicates a correlational relationship. This relationship only points out that the variables occur together in some specified manner, without implying that the one causes the other.

In the case of causal hypothesis there is an implication that the existence of, or a change in one variable causes or leads to an effect on the other variable. These two variables are described as independent and dependent variables. These may be characterized as 'if-then' relationships, which means that if a particular condition exists in the independent variable, then a predictable consequence will follow in the dependent variable.

According to Emory and Cooper,

> there are two approaches of hypothesis testing. The more established is the classical or 'sampling theory' approach, the second is known as the Bayesian approach. The classical approach is found in all of the major statistics books and is widely used in research applications. This approach represents an objective view of probability in which the decision making rests totally upon an analysis of available sampling data. A hypothesis is established, which is then rejected or fails to be rejected, based on the sample data collected. The Bayesian approach (based on Bayes Theorem) is an extension of the classical approach. It also uses sampling for making decisions, but it goes beyond this to consider all other information that is available. This additional information consists of scientific probability estimates stated in terms of degrees in belief. These subjective estimates are based on general experience rather than on specific collected data. They are expressed as a prior distribution that can be revised after gathering sample information. The revised estimate, known as posterior distribution, may be further revised by additional information, and so on. Various decision rules are established, cost and other estimates can be introduced, and the expected outcomes of combinations of these elements are used to judge decision alternatives.[6]

Two kinds of hypotheses are used in the classical type of

testing: the null and the alternative hypotheses. The null hypothesis is used for testing. It is the statement that no difference exists between the parameter and the statistic being compared to it. The alternative hypothesis is the logical opposite of the null hypothesis.

On the basis of the level of abstraction broadly three kinds of hypotheses may be distinguished:

(1) The most exact and least abstract, as they state the existence or presence of empirical uniformities.
(2) More complex, and they aim at testing the existence of logically derived relationship between empirical uniformities.
(3) Abstract, which are concerned with the relation of analytic variables.

It is important to note that the researcher has to go through the two processes of deduction and induction for developing any hypotheses. Deduction is the process which goes from the general to the specific. When general expectations about events based on presumed relationships between variables are used to arrive at more specific expectations or anticipated observations, that process is called deduction. In the inductive process we go from concrete to the abstract, that is, the inferences and generalizations are made on the basis of observation and analysis of empirical data leading to the development of theory. These two processes are not mutually exclusive, and both are helpful for the advancement of knowledge.

Based on the preceding examination of the types of hypotheses in the research process, a usable hypothesis should have the following characteristics when it is formulated: (1) The concept should be clear. (2) It should have empirical background. (3) It must be specific and predictions indicated should be spelled out. (4) The possibility of actual testing of the hypotheses can be approved. (5) It should be related to a body of theory and should possess theoretial relevance. (6) It should be related to available techniques. (7) It should be conceivable and not absurd; it must be capable of being brought into an accepted body of knowledge.

According to R.P. Misra,

> A very essential element in the method of hypothesis is known as the process of the hypothesis. This involves two things. In the first place a

good hypothesis is usually the product of a number of relatively vague guesses fused together by a process of elimination of the irrelevant ideas, and a reconstruction of what are left into a clear and definite hypothesis. In the second place, the hypothesis must also be shaped to fit the facts. By moulding is meant the process of using vague and indefinite ideas into the clear and precise principles of explanation, formulated so as to fit the facts under consideration and relevant to the problem. It must be emphasised that even though the hypothesis has been moulded to fit the facts it is not verified. It only becomes a working hypothesis to be established possibly by further investigation.

He further states that there are some important conditions that are conducive to the formulation of a hypotheses. First, it must be so formulated that deduction is possible and consequently, a decision reached as to whether or not it does explain the facts considered; second, it should provide the answer to the problem which generated the enquiry; third, it should provide facts (from observations or test) which would reveal certain propositions to be true, whose truths are known at the time; and fourth, it must be simple and help eliminate irrelevant facts.[7]

In short, a good hypothesis is the keystone of empirical research. It enables the researcher to articulate propositions for testing and describes relationships between or among variables. A good hypothesis can explain, what it claims to explain, it is testable and has greater range, probability and simplicity than the alternative propositions. Hypotheses also play an important role in collecting, analysing and interpreting data, and in the development of theory.

NOTES

1. *Webster's International Dictionary of the English Language*, 1956.
2. W.L. French and C.H. Bell, *Organisation Development*, Prentice Hall of India Pvt. Ltd., New Delhi, 1983, p. 92.
3. Dommer, Daniel, Robinson, *The Principles of Reasoning*, D. Appleton Century Co. Inc., USA, 1936, p. 236.
4. C. Selltiz, M. Jahoda, M. Deutsch, S.W. Cook, *Research Methods in Social Relations*, Holt, Rinehart and Winston Inc., USA, 1961, p. 35.
5. T.S. Wilkinson, and P.L. Bhandarkar, *Methodology and Techniques of Social Research*, Himalaya Publishing House, Bombay, 1979, p. 65.
6. W.C. Emory and D.R. Cooper, *Business Research Methods*, Richard D. Irwin, Inc., Homewood, Illinois, 1991, pp. 519-20.
7. R.P. Misra, *Research Methodology*, Concept Publishing Company, New Delhi, 1989, pp. 22-7.

CHAPTER 7

Methods of Data Collection

The most important element in the quality of research is data and may be described as the foundation on which the entire edifice of a research study rests. The quality of data, therefore, ultimately determines the quality of generalizations, abstractions, and inferences through which a theory is built or supported. The choice of methods of data collection determines to a considerable extent the nature and characteristics of the data, and their validity and reliability. Since data collection is largely a subjective process, there are risks of distortions and bias, which may affect their quality and in turn the quality of research findings. As pointed out by Selltiz, Jahoda, and others, the purpose of various data collection techniques is to produce trustworthy evidence that is relevant to the research questions being asked. The purpose of the accompanying rules is to facilitate the use of these data in making specific statements about the characteristics of the phenomenon to which the data are believed to be relevant.[1] In this chapter we will discuss the various methods of data collection, keeping in view their relevance to the fields of music and other performing arts.

Data collection is the process of noting and recording of materials concerning the researcher's subject of enquiry. It can be defined as one of the many research tools used in collecting useful information that is relevant from the researcher's point of view. Such information can be collected either from documentary or field sources. While documentary data are obtained from published or unpublished documents. The documentary data are contained in published or unpublished documents, and the field data are gathered from the persons who have fund of knowledge about or have been in intimate contact with, conditions and changes over a considerable period of time and who can describe not only the existing state of affairs but also the observable trends and significant milestones in that process.[2]

In the opinion of Whitney, data are the things with which we think. They are the raw material of reflection, until by comparison, combination and evaluation, they are stepped up to a higher level of generalization, where again they serve as basic material for further and higher thinking.[3]

Thus data collection is one of the most critical and central processes in any research study. Whereas the conceptual framework of research provides the blueprint, the data and information provide the foundation and the main body of the research. Therefore, the quality of data and the process of its collection are vital for any research study. Very often researchers spend considerable amount of time in exploring the existing theoretical writings on the subject of their study, many of which are subjective impressions and armchair speculations of the writers. In comparison, much less attention and time is given to identifying and collecting the primary and secondary data which can lead to deeper and fresh insights, and development of better quality of theory and knowledge.

The importance of carefully planning the collection of data probably seems most obvious and apparent. For data collection to be meaningful, there needs to be theoretical justification for the concepts used. This will ensure that data collection is based on concepts, which are found or believed to be related and hence the data collected will be more than just information to classify.[4]

It is always advisable for the researcher not to be in a hurry to conduct field search; instead, he/she should first consult the necessary documentary sources. These types of data can be collected through observation, personal interviews and mailed questionnaires, etc. Documentary data can be gathered from bibliographies, periodicals, abstracts, directories and yearbooks, encyclopaedias, dictionaries, etc. It would be useful for the researcher to be aware of the important documentary sources in the subject area before setting out for the field search. Documentary data are mostly available in libraries, archives and sometimes with individuals and involve no fieldwork but only the effort of finding the relevant records.

There are two major sources that provide two types of data: (a) Primary, and (b) Secondary. Primary sources are gathered at first hand, and secondary ones are those from which data can be collected second hand. 'The primary data are those which are collected afresh and for the first time and thus happen to be original in character. The secondary data, on the other hand, are those which have already been collected by someone else and which have already been passed through statistical process.'[5]

Data may be further characterized by their (1) abstractness, (2) verifiability, (3) elusiveness, and (4) closeness to the phenomenon. As abstraction, data are more metaphorical than real. Second, data are processed by human senses, often limited in comparison to other living organisms. When sensory experiences consistently produce the same result, the data are said to be trustworthy, as they can be verified. Third, collection of data is complicated by the speed at which events occur and the time bound nature of observation. Opinions, preferences, and attitudes vary from one milieu to another, and with the passage of time. Finally, data classify their verity by closeness to the phenomena. Secondary data have had at least one level of interpretation inserted between the event and its recording. Primary data are sought for their proximity to the truth and control error. These characteristics caution researchers to use care in designing data collection procedures and generalizing from results.[6]

Data may also be classified as quantitative or qualitative. The quantitative data have greater possibility of accuracy and are easier to analyse for the purpose of testing the hypothesis. The qualitative data, although relatively difficult to measure and analyse, usually have possibilities in terms of making important inferences, and providing insightful generalizations. These two types of data are not mutually exclusive, and may reinforce each other in improving the quality of research.

It has been observed by writers on research methodology that data exhibit different levels of generalization. They may be either highly subjective or almost objective. And this is found to be so in the fields of natural sciences, and in the realm of human values and activities. They are either quantitative or qualitative, attributes or variables, and may also be classified by the methods and types of research employed by the researcher.

A wide variety of methods and techniques of data collection have been developed for collecting data from the primary and secondary sources. These range from survey of existing research studies and relevant literature to fieldwork utilizing various techniques like observation, interviews, questionnaire surveys, experimental design, case study, etc. These methods have been classified into different categories, which are often contradictory and sometimes confusing.

Lundberg points out that the methods of gathering data should be distinguished from methods of manipulating, summarizing, generalizing or otherwise handling data already collected. It is true that the possible ways of handling data after they are collected are largely determined by the method employed in their collection and, therefore, our model of collection must be governed to a large degree by the method of handling, which we plan to employ. But much of the confusion and argument over the current classifications of 'methods' is due to the failure of distinguishing between methods of gathering and that of classification, treatment and manipulation. Thus we have the historical method, the 'case' method, the 'statistical' method and 'survey' method, etc. There is nothing new or mutually exclusive in these classifications. From one point of view, all collections of data are collections of 'cases'. The survey method is a type of investigation with reference to scope, and may utilize any or all methods of collecting data. A useful classification of the methods of gathering data, like all classifications, must specify, first, the basis or purpose of the classification; and second, its categories must be mutually exclusive.[7]

To start the process of data collection, it is important to not only decide the method and tools of data gathering, but also the nature and size of the sample to be studied, because it is generally not always possible to collect information about the entire population in a given field of study. The entire population is only covered in a census study.

Sampling

The basic idea of sampling is that some of the elements in a population provide useful information on the entire population. Deming argues that the quality of a study is often better with sampling than with a census. He suggests 'sampling possesses the possibility of better interviewing (testing), more thorough investigation of missing, wrong or suspicious information, better supervision, and better processing than is possible with complete coverage'.[8] It is important, however, that the sample be truly representative of the population from which it is drawn. A good sample must be valid, i.e. it represents the characteristics of the population that it purports to represent. The criteria of a good sample are: accuracy, defined as the degree to which bias is absent from the sample; and precision, that is the degree to which it reflects the characteristics of the population with the least error.

The size of sample should be chosen carefully, for which some statistical methods and judgement of experts may be helpful to ensure that it is suitably representative of the population. Further, the researcher should keep in mind the possibility of statistical treatment of data for analysis and the generalizability of the findings from data.

Different sampling techniques may be utilized after determining a suitable sample size. Briefly, these techniques may be described as probability sampling and non-probability sampling. In probability sampling the commonly used methods are random sampling, stratified sampling and cluster sampling. In non-probability sampling, practical considerations, such as limitations of time and resources are taken into account, and the sample is, therefore, determined subjectively on the basis of the considered judgement of the researcher, usually in consultation with experts or persons knowledgeable about the subject. According to this method one can choose the purposive or convenience sampling method. The purposive sample conforms to certain criteria, which are based on the judgement of the researcher. And is also called judgement sampling. Another type of purposive sample is the quota sample, in which an attempt is made to ensure that the sample represents the particular characteristics of the subgroups of the population that it represents.

Another non-probability sample, that is often utilized, is the convenience sample. Such a sample is the least reliable in research design, but is normally the cheapest and easiest to conduct. In this case the researchers or fieldworkers are given the freedom to choose and include in the sample whomsoever they find relevant for the study.

Literature Survey

Knowledge, as we know, is a constantly developing phenomenon, which has its roots in the thoughts, insights, theories and research findings, of a large number of people, and is documented in the written form in books, periodicals, theses, manuscripts and other sources available in libraries. A researcher, who proposes to study a particular subject and advance the frontiers of knowledge through research, must be reasonably familiar with the existing state of knowledge in that area. It is, therefore, essential that those engaged in research must be thoroughly familiar with the previous body of research work done in their subject area through a careful study of relevant existing literature. For this purpose a review of literature is necessary as the starting point of a proposed study. According to Borg and Gall 'the literature in any field forms the foundation upon which all future work will be built. If we fail to build the foundation of knowledge provided by the review of literature, our work is likely to be shallow and naive and will often duplicate work that has already been done better by someone else.'[9]

The review of related literature requires the systematic identification, location and study of documents containing information related to the research problem. Such review enables the researcher to determine the work that has already been done relating to his/her subject. It also helps in identifying possible research strategies, specific procedures and measuring instruments that have been found useful or otherwise in investigating the problem.

The literature survey not only provides the foundation for further study but also avoids the risk of repeating the work already done. It can help in understanding the existing theories, ideas, explanations or hypotheses, which in turn can be useful in specifying the scope and focus of the new study and proposing new hypotheses. It may further help in providing insights and evaluating the strengths and limitations of the previous studies and to improve the present research study.

As stated earlier, the review of literature should be conducted at three levels. The first level includes the general sources, which provide clues to location of references of a general nature on a topic. These sources may include media reports, encyclopaedias, reference books, and other guides to periodical literature, etc.

Such sources provide a general overview of and introduction to a topic. The second level of review would require going through the secondary sources directly related to the subject of study, such as the books on the subject, reviews of research, textbooks, anthologies of readings, etc. Finally, based on the primary sources, the researcher must also study the researches done on the subject. Such studies are available in journals, abstracts and scholarly books, and reported theses and dissertations containing original reports of the fieldwork. It is now possible to have access to the above sources through the electronic media such as the World Wide Web and the Internet by using a computer. (This new source of information is discussed in detail in Chapter 9 of this book.)

It is advisable for the researcher to prepare a bibliography of published material, that may be relevant for the literature survey and further study on the subject simultaneously with the review of literature. The bibliography not only facilitates in locating references during the study, but also avoids the various problems, which may arise at the time of the completion of a research report or thesis.

Observational Methods

Observation is a natural human process in which we are continuously engaged as we experience life, the events around us, and nature. It is the basic method of obtaining information about the world around us. Observation becomes a scientific technique of data collection for research when it is planned systematically to serve a formulated research purpose, is recorded carefully, and related to more general propositions. And rather than being presented merely as a set of interesting phenomena, is subjected to scientific checks and controls on its validity and reliability.

There are several areas of information for which observation is the only available method and in which the data required by the researcher can be obtained through direct observation. In a sense scientific knowledge begins with observation and must ultimately return to observation for its final validation.

In fields related to human behaviour, observation may be defined as 'systematic viewing coupled with consideration of the seen phenomena'. It is more than merely viewing things as it involves seeing closely and purposely at the situation as a whole. In addition to visual data, it may include listening, reading, and the senses of smell and touch. Observation includes the full range of monitoring verbal, non-verbal, behavioural and non-behavioural activities and conditions. Thus, observation comprises the recording of data as they come to the investigator's notice in which he/she plays a largely passive role.

Observation involves three distinguishable components: sensation, attention, and perception. Sensation is gained through the sense organs, which depends upon the physical alertness of the observer. Then comes attention or concentration, which is largely a matter of will power, but adequate training, and experience can make it almost a matter of habit. Third is perception, which comprises the interpretation of sensory reports. Thus, sensation merely reports the facts as observed but perception enables the mind to recognize the facts. Through this process, observation serves the purpose of (i) studying collective behaviour and complex situations; (ii) following up of individual units comprising the situation; (iii) understanding the whole and the parts in their interrelation; and (iv) getting out of the way details of the situation.[10]

Observational method is in some cases the only method available for study, such as in the case of populations in which the survey or experimentation method cannot be utilized. An advantage of this method is that the original data can be collected as it occurs, therefore it avoids the filtration of information by respondents, and eliminates the factor of forgetting by respondents in the data based on questioning. Another strength of this method is that we can secure information that most participants in a survey would ignore either because it is so common and expected or because it is not seen as relevant. A unique advantage of observation is that only with this method can a research capture the whole event as it occurs in its natural environment. Finally, experience shows that subjects being studied seem to accept an observational type of intrusion better than questioning. It is less demanding of them and normally has a less biasing effect on their conduct than does questioning.

There are, however, some limitations of the observational method, which must be taken into account. First, the observer must be at the scene of the event, where it takes place, which may or may not be predicted in advance. Observation is a slow and expensive process that requires either human observers or some type of costly recording equipment. Second, the most reliable results are restricted to data that can be determined by observable action or surface indicators. To go below the surface, the observer must make inferences. Third, the research environment is more likely suited to subjective assessment and recording of data than controls and quantification of events. Furthermore, even with small sample sizes, the records of observation can be disproportionately large and difficult to analyse. Finally, it is difficult to gather information on intentions, attitudes, opinions, or preferences of individuals through this method. In spite of such limitations, any consideration of the merits of observation indicates that it is a valuable research tool when used with care and understanding.[11]

It may be emphasized here that the observational method has great relevance in the context of research in the field of music, because of it being a performing art. Unlike other methods of research which depend heavily on narrow quantification and other limitations, the observational method enables a wholistic study of performing arts in their socio-cultural context. The observation method is, therefore, particularly suited and recommended for research in performing musical forms and traditions, including vocal, instrumental, and dance. Similarly, it is equally relevant for the study of the dramatics, and fine arts.

The observational methods can be classified as follows: (a) non-controlled and (b) controlled. Further, both these types can be subdivided into two categories: (a) non-participant observation and (b) participant observation. The non-controlled observation refers to unstructured observation, whereas controlled observation refers to structured and standardized observational techniques. Further, the environment can be controlled by the researcher through a degree of structure imposed on it. Thus, the environment can consist of a natural setting, or a controlled laboratory environment.

The non-participant observation refers to a research method in which the researcher does not participate in group activities being observed, and does not pretend to be a member of the group being observed. The observer usually chooses a spot, where his presence is least disturbing to the group, but from where he/she can observe in detail the behaviour of individuals and the group under observation.

The participant observation refers to the method in which the researcher becomes a regular participant in the group's activities being observed and his dual role of being a participant and the researcher at the same time may or may not be known to the other participants. Thus he gets a closer and better understanding and feel of the various processes and activities of the group and their meaning to the members of the group. This method has been widely used for research in cultural anthropology, and has been found to be more reliable, flexible and more searching than surveys and questionnaires, because it discloses many hidden and delicate details not accessible to other methods. However, it may in some cases suffer from the disadvantage of the participant observer losing his/her sense of objectivity.

The following is a brief description of the combinations of the above methods of observation:

(i) Non-Controlled and Non-Participant Observation: This method refers to a study of social situation as it exists from outside without participating in the social life of the people being observed. In such studies the researcher observes not only the total context and physical aspects but also the social atmosphere and details of other behavioural phenomena. Often such observations are made over a long period of time by the researchers as a passive observer in the hope of obtaining more reliable data.

(ii) Non-Controlled Participant Observation: This method has a tendency to supply naturalness and completeness of behaviour in a given situation and allows sufficient time to observe it. Since the period of participation may continue for a long duration, the range of materials collected will be much wider and enables the investigator to record the context, which gives meaning to expressions of opinions. In the case of non-controlled observations, the investigator must consciously apply a range of tools for systematizing and recording of data. The investigator

should carry on the analysis, as it is profitable to record both observation and interpretation of the observation simultaneously.

(iii) Controlled Participant Observation: Under this method, the investigator becomes a member of the group he is observing, but replaces passive observation with specific categories, like vague impressions of body build by anthropometrical measurements, guesses about distances with the help of exact maps, and other similar criteria of measurement. In controlled observation, the formal interview, the inventory or schedule and map exercise control over the observer. In this case, the investigator tries to systematize the process of observation. Controlled observation limits the bias of the individual observer.

(iv) Controlled Non-Participant Observation: A controlled non-participant observation method was applied by Robert F. Bales of the Harvard University for his study entitled 'Interaction Process Analysis: A Method for the Study of Small Groups'. In this study Bales relied primarily on the objective observation of small problem solving groups, and was interested in the interaction process itself, the role of each test participant in this process, and the interrelationships among these roles. In other words, he wanted to know how the inter-stimulations were derived by various members of the test group. On the basis of preliminary observations, in order to obtain data on patterns of interaction, uniformities in action, and their frequencies, he set out certain categories. Then through various mechanical devices the data were obtained.[12] This method can be extended to other situations for research by pre-determining and categorizing the behaviour to be observed, and the researcher taking a non-membership role in the group being observed.

The Questionnaire

The questionnaire as a tool of data collection is one of the most popular methods used by researchers in social and behavioural studies. Unlike the observation method which restricts the collection of data to the behaviour and events as they occur, and provides information limited to the observable level, the questionnaire enables the researcher to probe people's feelings, attitudes, perceptions, motivation, aspirations, beliefs and values.

The questionnaire consists of carefully worded set of questions in a given area to elicit responses from a group of people. A well-designed questionnaire is a convenient, economical and a relatively quick method of obtaining data from a fairly large population. Further, it can provide data which can be analysed statistically for descriptive as well as analytical research.

The use of a questionnaire assumes that respondents are willing to help, and would give honest answers to the questions. That their stated responses would be a true reflection of their views, attitudes or beliefs, etc., sought to be measured. Further, that the respondents are knowledgeable about the subject and can articulate their views as required for the questionnaire. The information so obtained has to meet the tests of validity and reliability.

The questionnaire method of collecting data has the following advantages: it is less expensive; requires less skills to administer than an interview or observation; can be mailed to a geographically widespread population; and requires minimum explanation. The questionnaire provides anonymity and confidentiality to the respondent as well as privacy and sufficient time to respond which can elicit frank and candid information. The pressure on respondents for immediate response is lesser than that of personal interview. The questionnaire can provide coverage of large samples and thus make the results more dependable and reliable. Besides, it enables collection of data from a large number of respondents at the same time, and thus data can be obtained both simultaneously and quickly. All these reasons make it a suitable method for conducting surveys.

The method however has several limitations which need to be kept in view. One of the main disadvantages of the questionnaire method is that the completion and return rate is much lower than that of contacting individuals personally to ask questions through an interview or telephonic contact. It is a general experience of researchers that the response rate of mailed questionnaires varies from 10 per cent to 40 per cent. One major drawback of the usual questionnaire is that it is only appropriate for well-educated subjects. Therefore, only a small percentage of the population can be reached through the questionnaire. Even the educated respondents are seldom motivated to fill up the questionnaire, as it takes considerable time and attention. Besides, many of the assumptions stated above may not be realistic and the information obtained may not be as valid and reliable as in the other methods.

Designing and Administering Questionnaires: Designing and administering questionnaires require knowledge and skill, without which it may not elicit correct information and co-operation of the respondents. A good questionnaire should be short, attractive and simple to respond. It should not make unreasonable demands on respondents, not have a 'hidden agenda', and should have carefully worded questions that can be answered easily and correctly. Questionnaires which have an attractive, professional and easy to understand format, combined with mail-back facility, are likely to get a better response. It should contain clear and explicit directions as to how it should be completed and returned. It is useful to have questions, which are objective, and are ordered from easy to difficult and from general to specific. Wherever necessary, examples should be provided to help respondents complete a questionnaire.

One good way to obtain information through questionnaire is by giving it to a relevant group of respondents collected together at one place and time. This ensures quick and certain response as compared to mailing the questionnaires. It is also advisable that the mailed sponsoring questionnaire is sent along with a good covering letter from the research institution explaining the importance of the study, soliciting cooperation, ensuring confidentiality, and a personalized approach, expressing appreciation to respondents for providing the information.

As pointed out by Selltiz, Jahoda and others, there are many factors that influence the response to a mailed questionnaire. Among the most important factors are: (1) sponsorship of the questionnaire; (2) attractiveness of the questionnaire format; (3) length of questionnaire; (4) nature of the accompanying letter requesting cooperation; (5) ease of filling out the questionnaire and mailing it back; (6) inducements offered to reply; (7) nature of the people to whom the questionnaire is sent; and (8) finally the fact that attractively designed questionnaires that are short, easy to fill out, simple to return, sponsored by a group with prestige, and presented in a context that motivates the respondent to cooperate are most likely to be returned.[13]

Types of Questionnaires: The questionnaire can be designed as a structured and standardized questionnaire or a less structured or unstructured questionnaire to obtain exploratory information. The structured questionnaires are those in which there are definite, concrete and predetermined questions. In order to ensure valid and reliable responses the questions are standardized through preliminary tests and statistical methods. The form of questions in such questionnaires is of an objective type, or 'closed', to which the response can be stated by 'yes' or 'no', or from a multiple choice of responses. Such questionnaires are considered highly structured because they limit the options available to the respondents and avoid the use of respondents' own words. It is easy to respond to these types of questionnaires and equally easy to process the obtained data, unlike the less structured and open-ended questions.

The questionnaire in which the questions are open-ended, and in which the above-mentioned characteristics are not present, can be termed as unstructured or less-structured questionnaire. Such questionnaires are helpful for obtaining exploratory data and develop working hypotheses. On the basis of such preliminary study, structured questionnaires can be designed. The processing of data so obtained is difficult and may require techniques like 'content analysis'. Therefore, open-ended questions should be used sparingly, and may be combined with the structured questionnaire to obtain qualitative information.

Formulation and Wording of Questions: The form and wording of questions is critical for obtaining the right response from the respondents. The researcher should ensure that each question is clear and free from any sort of misunderstanding and ambiguity that may distort the data. Questions should be impartial and stated in a manner, that does not offend the respondent or give a biased view. Each question should have only one specific query and should not combine more sub-questions. Questions should be asked in a manner that may make it easy and clear to answer accurately. The element of 'social desirability' should be kept in view and, therefore, questions to which the subjects will respond with such bias must be avoided. Questions should be constructed with a view to their forming a logical part of a well thought out tabulation plan. In general all questions should meet the following standards: (a) should be easily understood; (b) should be simple, i.e. conveying only one thought at a time; (c) should be concrete and; (d) should conform as much as possible to the respondent's way of thinking.[14]

The wordings of questions are also very important, as reliable and meaningful responses depend on them to a large extent. Simple words, which are familiar to all respondents, should be chosen. Ambiguous and complex words should be avoided; and words with emotional connotations should also not be used. The main point to be kept in mind is that the wording should not bias the answer. For designing the questionnaire, it is an advisable approach to cross-check the meaning of the questions as understood by the respondents through a pilot study. There are several statistical techniques, which can be utilized to standardize the questionnaire, and test its validity and reliability.

Interview Method

Interview is one of the most effective and widely utilized techniques for obtaining meaningful information for research. Several aspects of social behaviour which cannot be enquired through questionnaires or observational methods can be probed through the interview. This method is the most appropriate technique for revealing information about complex, emotionally laden subjects or for probing the sentiments that may underlay an expressed opinion. The flexibility of the interview method makes it a far superior technique for the exploration of areas where there is little basis for knowing, either what questions to ask or how to formulate them. In addition, the interviewing situation offers a better opportunity than the questionnaire to appraise validity of reports. The interviewer is in a position to observe not only what the respondent says but also how he says it.[15]

Personal interviewing is a two-way conversation initiated by an interviewer to obtain information from a respondent. The differences in roles of interviewer and respondent are pronounced. They are typically strangers, and the interviewer generally controls the topics and pattern of discussion. The consequences of the event are usually minimal to the respondent. The respondent is asked to provide information with little hope of receiving any immediate or direct benefit from this co-operation. Yet if the interview is carried off successfully, it is an excellent data collection technique.[16]

Interview as a method of data collection has several real advantages as well as limitations. Its strongest point is the depth and detail of information that can be obtained. In this respect it is a much superior method compared to questionnaires, surveys and observation. A skilful and trained interviewer can obtain valuable and insightful information, and can probe many unexplored areas through the interview.

The interviewer also has more control than with other kinds of exploration. He can adjust the language of the interview by observing the impact that the interviews are having on the respondents. Further, the interviewer can be selective and ensure that the correct respondent is chosen for interview, and can set up and control interviewing conditions. It is also possible to use special scoring device, visual materials, etc., to elicit more authentic responses.

Unlike the questionnaires, which can be used only with an educated population, interviews can be used with almost all segments of the population. People are generally more willing to cooperate in a study in which they are asked to give their views orally. It also offers the possibility of repeating or rephrasing questions to make sure that they are understood clearly, and of asking further questions in order to clarify the meaning of responses to questions. An interview is likely to be more successful in creating an atmosphere that allows the respondent to express feelings, or to report behaviours that are customarily disapproved. These characteristics of the interview method make it a highly effective technique for data collection.

Although interview as a technique has several advantages

as stated above, it also has some constraints and limitations. One of the major reasons why this method cannot be used widely in most researches is that it is costly both in terms of money and time. A personal interview is not only costly but also full of problems especially in arranging contacts and obtaining appointments from hard-to-reach persons. The recording of information obtained through interviews and reporting it correctly is also not easy. This method requires a high degree of skill and training without which there is a possibility of bias and distortion of information. The analysis of data obtained through this method also poses several problems, because of the complexity and volume of information so obtained.

The conditions that can make a personal interview successful are the ability of the interviewer to establish a rapport and gain confidence of the interviewees; availability of the needed information from the respondents; respondents' understanding of their role; and adequate motivation for them to cooperate.

Interview Technique: Interviewing for research is a complex process, which requires considerable skill. What the interviewer says or does can make or break a study. Respondents often react, more in terms of their feelings towards the interviewer than to the content of the questions. It is also important that the interviewer asks the questions properly, records the responses accurately, and probes meaningfully. To achieve these aims, the interviewer must be trained to carry out those procedures that foster a good interviewing relationship.

The first goal in an interview is to establish a friendly relationship with the respondent. Three factors will help to bring about respondent receptiveness. The respondent must: (1) feel that the experience will be pleasant and satisfying; (2) believe that the survey is important and worthwhile; and (3) have any mental reservations satisfied. In the successful interview there is rapport, meaning that a relationship of confidence and understanding exists between the interviewer and the respondent. Interview situations are often new to respondents, and they need help in defining their roles. The interviewer can help by conveying the fact that the interview is confidential and important, and that the respondent can discuss the topics with freedom from censure, coercion or pressure. Under such conditions, the respondent can obtain much satisfaction in opening up without pressure being exerted.[17]

Recording the Interview: There are several ways in which information obtained through interviews can be recorded, but the most commonly used method is to write down the answers of the respondent during the interview. Since it is difficult to memorize the information given by the interviewee, it is important to record responses as they take place. The interviewer could use some system of shorthand that will record the essence of the respondent's replies. The use of key words would be helpful for this purpose.

The interviewer can also repeat the response while writing it down. This practice cross-checks the interviewer's understanding of the response, and sustains the respondent's interest. It is helpful to seek the approval of the respondent for taking notes and especially if the interview is being recorded on a tape recorder. The interviewer should start taking notes as soon as the respondent begins to reply.

Another method of recording such data is through recall immediately after the interview. This method has some limitations, but may be necessary in some situations.

Telephone Interviewing: Telephone interviewing has become a widely used technique as it is economical and efficient. Through this method it is possible to reach a large and widely spread population in a short time. However, it lacks personal touch and rapport that can be developed in the personal interview. Some respondents also resent telephonic interviews and the responses are not as good as in the personal interview. Telephonic interview can be more helpful in setting up personal interviews, and screening large populations for selecting interviewees. Further, it can be a good follow-up technique for more information after a personal interview, and is a good device to improve the response rate of mail surveys by making prior notification and follow-up calls to respondents.

Types of Interviews: Broadly, interviews can be classified into two types: structured and unstructured interviews. Structured interviews involve the use of a set of pre-determined questions and standardized techniques of recording. The interviewer follows a pre-determined procedure, asking questions in a form and order which is already laid down. In comparison, the unstructured interviews are based on a flexible approach to questioning. The interviewer is allowed greater freedom to ask supplementary questions, if needed, or to omit some questions depending on the requirements of the situation. Further, the interviewer may change the sequence of questions or probe the responses for a better understanding. The unstructured interviews are especially helpful in exploratory researches or formulative stages of the research studies.

In addition to the above, forms of interviews other types such as the 'focused', 'clinical', and 'non-directive' interviews are also utilized for specific purposes. The focused interview aims at confining the respondent to a discussion of an issue that the researcher seeks to study. This approach is generally utilized in the development of hypothesis. The clinical interview can also be described as a depth interview to study the motivations and deeper feelings or experiences in an individual's life experiences. The non-directive interview is a special technique in which the interviewer plays a passive role and encourages the respondent to express his thoughts and feelings freely. The interviewer asks very few direct questions and facilitates the process by active listening and empathy. The interviewer may also paraphrase or restate his understanding of the thoughts and feelings of the interviewee. This method of interview can elicit deep feelings, and is also utilized for therapy.

Schedule and Check-list

These devices are utilized for conducting structured or semi-structured interviews, specially in researches in which the information desired is clearly defined as in the case of descriptive research like census, and in situations in which all respondents may not be able to fill up the questionnaire. These devices are used by trained fieldworkers to collect data by asking questions and recording the responses as specified in the schedule or check-list for interview. This method ensures a high level of response compared to the personal interview and mailed questionnaire.

CASE STUDY METHOD

As contrasted with the survey method through which the researcher draws generalizations based on data collected from a sizeable sample, the case study method is utilized for in-depth understanding of an individual, an institution or a social unit, like a family, tribe, or community. It may be defined as a method used to study an individual or an institution in a unique setting or situation in as intense and as detailed a manner as possible.[18]

The aim of this method is to find out the factors that account for the behaviour patterns of the given unit and its relationships with the environment. The case data are always gathered with a view to tracing the natural history of the social unit and its relationships with the social factors and the forces involved in its surrounding milieu. In sum, through the case study method, the social researcher attempts to understand the complex of factors that are operative within a social unit as an integrated totality.[19]

The essential procedure of the case study method is to take account of all pertinent aspects of a thing or situation, employing as the unit for study an individual, an institution, a community, or any group considered as a unit. The case consists of the data relating to some phase of the life history of the unit or relating to the entire life process, whether the unit is an individual, a family, a social group, an institution or a community. The complex situation and combination of factors involved in the given behaviour are examined to determine the existing status and to identify the causal factors in operation.[20]

This method is used extensively in the fields of medicine, management, anthropology and psychology. The pioneering work of Sigmund Freud on the psychoanalytic theory of personality development was based on case studies of his patients. Similarly, cultural anthropologists, sociologists and researchers in the field of management have done some highly significant case studies.

The case study method has several strong points: it focuses on only one entity which allows for very close examination and scrutiny and the collection of a great volume of detailed data. It encourages the use of several different techniques to get the necessary information, ranging from personal observations, interviews to written documents and records. It has been rightly said that there is simply no way to get a richer account of what is occurring in a particular entity, than through a case study. The case study, therefore, suggests directions for further studies, although it may not necessarily result in hypotheses being tested. It is for these reasons that case studies have always been popular as a method in clinical setting.[21]

There are some shortcomings and controversial viewpoints about the usefulness of the case study method for research. Although it may appear easy on surface, it is one of the most time consuming research methods. Second, the possibility of bias of the researcher is much higher in this method than in other methods. Third, what the case studies provide in depth, they lose in breadth. Fourth, the method does not provide sufficient data for generalizing the findings and establishing cause and effect relationship. Some scientists believe that case studies will never result in ground-breaking basic research (which is not their purpose in any case). Case studies do, however, reveal a diversity and richness of human behaviour that is simply not accessible through any other method.[22]

Data Collection in Music

The field of music in general and Indian music in particular has some unique characteristics because of which the methods of data collection have to be chosen carefully. From the preceding discussion of the methods of data collection, it is evident that the method of observation, interview and case study have special relevance for the study of music and performing arts. Indian music has strong oral traditions, dating back to centuries. It also has the unique *gharana* and *sampraday* system, which has no parallel anywhere else in the world. Any attempt to study Indian music would require great sensitivity and understanding of these two characteristic traditions of the system of Indian music.

The research studies regarding the various practices and styles of music in the *gharanas* necessitate the use of data collection methods like observation and case study. In order to appreciate and understand the subtle differences and characteristics of the musical traditions in a particular *gharana*, a researcher may have to follow a step-by-step approach of beginning as a non-participant observer. For a deeper study he/ she may have to establish a closer rapport and even enter the *gharana* as a participant observer. The researcher could also choose the case study and interview methods to explore the various facets of the subject.

Similarly, because of the very strong oral traditions in Indian music, a research study of the subject may require intensive and skilful use of the interview and observation methods. It appears that the interview method is especially suited for the study of Indian music, as is evident from the large number of research studies of music that have used this method.

However, it may be emphasized here that the interview method has to be handled with considerable patience, skill and sensitivity. It may take a long time for a researcher to establish rapport with the artistes, and a great deal of skill to gain their confidence so that the artistes may share and reveal the deeper intricacies of the art. Besides these well-known methods of data collection, research in the field of music and performing arts requires some non-traditional and novel sources of information which have special relevance and significance in such studies. These sources include sculptures, paintings, frescoes, manuscripts, oral traditions, etc., which will be examined in detail in the following chapters.

NOTES

1. C. Selltiz, M. Jahoda, M. Deutsch and S.W. Cook, *Research Methods in Social Relations*, Holt, Rinehart and Winston, Inc., USA, 1961, p. 147.
2. V.M. Palmer, *Field Studies in Sociology*, University of Chicago Press, 1928, p. 57.
3. F.L. Whitney, *The Elements of Research*, Prentice Hall, Inc., New York, 1954, p. 133.
4. P.H. Rigby, *Conceptual Foundations of Business Research*, John Wiley and Sons, New York, 1965.
5. C.R. Kothari, *Research Methodoloy: Methods and Techniques*, Wiley Eastern Ltd., New Delhi, 1985.
6. C.W. Emory and D.R. Cooper, *Business Research Methods*, Richard D. Irwin, Homewood, Illinois, 1991, p. 89.
7. G.A. Lundberg, *Social Research: A Study in Methods of Gathering Data*, Longman, Green and Co., New York, 1929, p. 85.
8. W.E. Deming, *Sample Design in Business Research*, John Wiley and Sons, New York, 1960, p. 26.

9. P.M. Borg and M.D. Gall, *Educational Research: An Introduction*, McGraw Hill Book Co., New York, 1967.
10. M.H. Gopal, *An Introduction to Research Procedures in Social Sciences*, Asia Publishing House, Bombay, 1970, p. 175.
11. See Emory and Cooper, op. cit., pp. 402-3.
12. See B.C. Tandon, *Research Methodology in Social Sciences*, Chaitanya Publishing House, Allahabad, 1987, p. 138.
13. C. Selltiz et al., op. cit., pp. 241-2.
14. C.R. Kothari, op. cit., p. 146.
15. See C. Selltiz et al., op. cit., p. 242.
16. Emory and Cooper, op. cit., p. 320.
17. Ibid., pp. 321-4.
18. N.J. Salkind, *Exploring Research*, Prentice Hall, New Jersey, 1997, p. 21.
19. T.S. Wilkinson, and P.L. Bhandarkar, op. cit., p. 243.
20. Carter V. Good and Douglas E. Scates, *Methods of Research*, Appleton Century Crofts, New York, 1954.
21. See N.J. Salkind, op. cit., p. 212.
22. Ibid., p. 213.

CHAPTER 8

Sources of Data for Research in Indian Music

As has been emphasized in the earlier chapters the sources which provide information and data in conducting any research are of great importance for a reliable study. The data required for any study depend upon the subject of the research, the nature of the problem to be studied, the methodology chosen and the researcher's interests and resources. The quality of any research depends on the authenticity and reliability of the sources utilized by the researcher. Therefore, before embarking on the research work, it is essential that the researcher be aware of the varied sources from which information and data can be obtained, and the veracity and reliability of such sources.

As we know, unlike other social sciences in which tangible statistical data can be obtained for measurement, the field of music is a performing art the outputs of which can be subjectively felt and appreciated and cannot be seen and easily measured in quantitative terms. Therefore, the methods of research in music have to be enlarged and adapted beyond those research in social sciences. Some of these methods may be quite unconventional and may depend on sources, seldom utilized in other social sciences.

It is well known that Indian music has largely depended for its continuity and development on the oral tradition rather than the written form. Consequently, several non-written forms of information such as paintings, sculptures, folklore, traditions in *gharanas*, compositions and subjective knowledge passed down the generations to the practising artistes, by their ancestors and *gurus* may be valuable sources of information. In this chapter an attempt will be made to identify and describe those sources of information which are uniquely suitable for research in music, particularly for Indian music.

SCULPTURE

The artistic forms of expression differ from country to country depending on the cultures that produce them; with each culture having a characteristic inclination towards specific modes of expression. On the basis of historical evidence the art historians hold the view that the genius of the people of India is basically sculptural.

The tradition of Indian sculpture is as old as the Indus Valley civilization. Excavations in Harappa and Mohenjo-daro (now in Pakistan in Sind) have revealed the existence of urban centres as far back as 2500 BC. In the words of Widyati Ro-esijadi, by and large, the great sculptural tradition of Eastern Asia was fertilized with seeds sown by Indians. Their approach towards the visual arts was always basically sculptural meaning that sculpture, architecture, and even painting were conceived in terms of palpable volumes. That most rewarding vehicle of the sculptor's art, the human body, was celebrated and affirmed in the substratum of primitive faith that predated both Hinduism and Buddhism, and this attitude was not only manifested but subtly exploited in the art of both later creeds.

The assertion that this unique attitude towards sculpture and the human body existed at the dawn of Indian history is verified by statuettes found among the remaining of the civilizations that flourished in the Indus Valley, however, there are scant remains of any type of artistic activity. The creative energy of that thousand years' span was dedicated not to the arts but to religion and philosophy, and it was then that the religious systems, that were to dominate all of Eastern Asia were formulated.[1]

Depicting the human body the Indian sculptor sought not to reproduce nature but to create forms parallel to nature. Greatly influenced by dance, he interpreted the body as a receptacle filled with breath and pulsating life, and attempted to render externally its inner sensations as they rose to the surface.

A much-discussed statuette of the period is the image of a dancing girl from Mohenjo-daro. Executed in bronze, of about four inches height this figure of a young girl in a half impudent posture (John Marshal, *Mohenjo-daro and Indus Civilization*, vol. I) shows deft artistic handling. It has been argued that the young girl is a representative of temple dancers, an institution not more ancient than the medieval Hindu temple. Whether the figure represents a temple dancer or a social entertainer, is of little significance; most importantly it is a work of art. The figure is nude except for a necklace and one arm, which is covered in a series of bangles. According to Stuart Piggot, her ornaments, and complicated coiffure suggest 'a sophisticated version of the female type known in the rough, schematised figurines in the Kulli culture, with her right wrist resting on the tilted hip, and the other arm hanging free to hold the bowl, this statuette is a triumph of details in linear terms. The dancing line suggests more than it states. The artist has relied more on his intuitive perception of the image than verisimilitude to nature.'[2] Similarly, one stone bust, possibly of a priest, dating from before 2000 BC, has been found, which resembles figures found in Mesopotamia. There are possibilities that the Indus Valley people may have travelled to Mesopotamia for trade, etc., because excavations reveal settlements ranging from simple farming communities to seaports developed for foreign trade, and two thriving capitals at Harappa and Mohenjo-daro.

After the spread of Buddhism the earliest examples of monumental Indian sculptures were produced. During the lifetime of the Buddha, and for two centuries after his death in 480 BC, his influence was mainly confined to a small area of north-east India. Early in the third century BC most of northern and central India was united under a single empire, known as the Mauryan Empire after Chandragupta Maurya. The third emperor of the Maurya Dynasty, Ashoka, converted to Buddhism. He erected a series of great pillars inscribed with edicts. Representing the official, imperial style of sculpture, these pillars of highly polished sandstone supported depictions of symbolic animals.

The long campaign produced some of the greatest monuments and the most magnificent sculpture the world had known. Some of the finest examples are the Buddhist and Hindu temples at Ellora, near Aurangabad. Among these superb displays of sculptural virtuosity, is the outstanding Hindu temple of Kailasanatha, a free-standing structure hewn out of solid rock between AD 760 and 800. Buddha was probably first depicted in human form sometime in the first century BC, though the earliest dateable sculptures were made after AD 100.

When the Buddha was transformed into God, the first sculptors depicted him as a preacher, with his audience carved to the same scale. But by the time the magnificent sculpture was produced in the fifth century the figure of the Buddha had been enormously enlarged. And it was in this era that the noblest sculptures of the Buddha were produced, embodying to perfection the Buddhist ideals of serenity and spiritual harmony.[3]

The most circumstantial information regarding the Indian schools of fine art, prior to Moghul times, is that given by Taranath, a Tibetan Lama, who wrote a history of Buddhism in AD 1608. The last chapter, on sculpture and painting, translated by W.T. Heeley, an Indian Civil Service officer, in the *Indian Antiquary,* vol. IV, p. 101, provides many important landmarks in Indian art history. He writes

> In former days human masters who were endowed with miraculous powers produced astonishing works of art. It is expressly stated in the *Vinaya-agama* and other works that the wall paintings, etc., of those masters were such as to be deceived by the likeness to the actual things depicted. For some centuries after the departure of the teacher many such masters flourished. After they had ceased to flourish, many masters appeared who were gods in human form; these erected the eight wonderful Chaityas of Magadha—the Mahabodhi, Manjushri-dun-Dubh-ishvara, etc. (the relic shrines marking the chief sacred places of Buddhism) and many other objects.[4]

The stupa of Sanchi, the greatest monument erected in central India, was built between 50 BC to AD 100. This stupa is 50 ft high and magnificently decorative. The sculptural decoration is concentrated on the gateways carved and adorned by graceful figures of Yakshis. Describing the beauty of Sanchi sculptures, Havell comments that these provide a most wonderful picture of Indian life and thought. We can see, also, how strongly the idea of the essential unity of creation has taken hold of the Indian mind. The Sanchi sculptures are entirely naturalistic in the treatment of the human form. As Ferguson says,

> All the men and women have acted in all times, and the success or the failure of the representation, may consequently be judged by the same rules as are applicable to the sculpture of any place or country. Notwithstanding this, the mode of treatment is so regional and local

that it is difficult to assign it to any exact position in comparison with the arts of Western world.[5]

It is noteworthy that on the western gate of the stupa some sculptures depict various musical instruments of that period like Vipanchi Veena, flutes and Mridangam.

Similarly, the Barhut stupa of the Sung dynasty considered the oldest includes several sculptures depicting dancers and various types of musical instruments. The orchestral scenes portray several artistes, playing stringed and wind instruments, accompanied by drums and bells. Some of these figures are so exquisitely sculpted that they are a testimony to the advancement of the art of that period. Gradually, two schools of sculpture developed during the Kushan period: Gandhara and Mathura. While the Gandhara School was inspired by foreign influences in its style, the Mathura school adapted its style from the indigenous sculptural tradition.

Another famous series of sculptures which represents early Indian society and history are those of Amravati, a Buddhist settlement on the banks of Krishna river in South India. These are attributed to the last-half of the second century AD. One of the best preserved of these is a sculptured slab from the base of a stupa. These figures are considered to be the most beautifully designed of those times.

The Amravati sculptures show the Buddha for the first time in Indian art, as a divine being receiving worship, but not as the Indian ideal of divinity. It is a transitional type. Besides, these sculptures are of great importance to scholars and researchers in the field of music, as innumerable musical instruments are depicted on the carved panels. Interestingly, an instrument, which is similar to the Rabab or Sarod, can also be seen in one of the series.

Simultaneously, the lower valleys of Krishna and Godavari became the centres of Buddhism in south India. The sculptures have been found at various places of this area, such as Nagarjunakonda, Alluru, and Gumadidurru. Some of the Nagarjunakonda creations are displayed at the Nagarjunakonda Museum and the National Museum, New Delhi.

After the establishment of the Gupta dynasty the finest flowering of the new rules in aesthetics was reached during the reign of Chandragupta II, by which time the Gupta empire covered much of northern India. It was in this period that what has come to be accepted as the Indian view of art was given its final form.

In AD 320, following five centuries of division, Chandragupta I was to unite north India and in so doing was to inaugurate the classic age of Indian art. Lasting for four hundred years, the Gupta period saw the establishment of canons of beauty that were to regulate the form of Buddha image ever afterward. Although the Guptas were Hindu, they supported Buddhism and as a result sculpture was produced during their reign in the service of both religions.[6]

The learned scholar J.P. Guha states that eulogies from Huan Tsang indicate that the plastic arts during the Gupta period kept pace with other aesthetic forms. The fulfilment and maturity that we notice in Gupta art followed from the healthy blend of critical activity and creative sensibility. The Gupta age brought to bear upon its aesthetic practice both intellectual and critical discipline. Iconography, painting, music and dancing developed as intellectual disciplines and principles governing the practice of fine arts were precisely formulated. A common alertness unified the fine arts in this age.

The aesthetic gestures (*mudras*), finger-plays and hand poses were further developed during this period. Most frequently used gestures were the Katakhasta, Lolahasta and Anjalihasta. The Katakhasta, symbolic of hand holding a lotus signifies communication. The Anjalihasta, or the gesture of devotion is indicated by two hands joined palm to palm. The Lolahasta, sometimes called Lambahasta or Gajahasta, signifying repose is represented by the hand hanging down, the arm being kept rigid.[7]

It has been rightly said that sculpture and painting cannot be understood without a knowledge of dancing, especially the classical Indian dance, in which postures of the body, gestures of hands and fingers, even the movement of neck and eyes, represent emotions, such as fear and love and, together, narrate a sequence of events. During the Gupta period this body language was transferred to sculpture and painting, so that the poses of statues and of the figures of the wall paintings which still adorn the caves of Ajanta are immensely theatrical elements in a dance drama. It is this sense of harmony, rhythm and movement, which gives to the art of the Guptas its extraordinary vitality.

Figures of the Buddha produced during this period are among the most impressive of the world's works of art. Buddha emerges from the hands of the sculptor as the god who is the origin of all things, half-ascetic, half-king and wholly noble. The face is majestic, sunk in deep meditation.[8]

The famous Hindu temple dedicated to Shiva was built at Ellora in the Deccan under the patronage of the Rashtrakuta Kings (AD 757 to 973). The entire complex is carved from solid rock. This is considered as an example of rock cut architecture in all respects; in its plan, harmony and unity. In the opinion of Ro-esijadi, 'In central India, the site of Ellura is unrivalled in its grandeur. The depiction of Shiva as Lord of the dance in Cave number XXI reflects the serenity of Gupta spirit, but the relief of Vishnu, depicted in the Das Avtara Cave, is more dynamic in conception.' The cave temple on the island of Elephanta, built around the same time as the Kailash at Ellora, is famous for its sculptural excellence. Believed to have been constructed in the seventh century AD, the cushion capitals of its pillars indicate their similarity to those of Ellora. The interior is noted for its sculptures, depicting the legend of Shiva. The Trimurti sculpture is very famous and has been the subject matter of endless commentaries.[9] Commenting in this regard, Havell states that it is difficult to compare the magnificent sculpture of Elephanta temple with any of the masterpieces of the West; for its plane of aesthetic thought, not entirely peculiar to India, but one in which Indian artistes were supreme (E.B. Havell, *A Handbook of Indian Art*, p. 85).

Southern India during the early medieval period was dominated by the art of the Pallava Kingdom (AD 600-750). The Pallava style dominated the two famous monuments, of Mamallapuram and Kailashnath at Kanchi. The finest Orissan sculptures can be seen in the great temples of Bhuvaneshwar, Konarak, Puri, etc., the period of their construction ranging between the eighth and the thirteenth centuries. The monumental horses and elephants and the erotic architectural sculptures of the Sun temple at Konarak are especially noteworthy. The magnificent temples of Khajuraho are literally covered with sculpture in a hard creamy sandstone, and isolated fine examples have been found at Mahoba, the Chandel capital. These temples are dedicated to Shiva, Vishnu and Jain patriarchs. The principal sculptures in Khajuraho temples are those of Ashtadikpalas (the regents of the eight quarters of the globe), Apsaras and Surasundaris (divine nymphs), Maithunas (erotic couples), Vidyadharas (flying celestials), and Nayikas (heroines). Referring to the double tier of graceful Apsaras of Vamana temple Stella Kramrisch has said, 'with every movement of the eye of the beholder a new perspective shows the images from a different angle; to avoid being bewildered, he has to concentrate on each of them, facing it, and then give his attention to the next'.[10]

An enormous revival in building work and sculpture took place in the Deccan under the later Chalukyas after AD 973, under the Hoysalas of Mysore in the twelfth and thirteenth centuries, and in Gujarat under the related Solanki dynasty (between the tenth and fifteenth centuries). The sculpture of the Deccan and Mysore is executed in a fine-grained dark chlorithic schist, which is comparatively soft when first queried, and lends itself to an unlimited elaboration of detail more appropriate to metalwork than stone. Almost all the work is of architectural application, and unbelievably rich in quantity and detail. Especially characteristic are the elevated temple basements, with tier upon tier of sculptured friezes, and the huge turned cylindrical pillars of the porches, with luxuriously developed bracket figures of dancers. Belur, Dodda Gadavalli, Somnathpur and Sravana Belagola are among the most famous sites in Mysore. The remarkable, 57 ft in height, monolithic image of Gommatesvara at Svavana Belagola is one of the largest free-standing figures in the world. Another figure in Ilivala is more than 20 ft in height.

In Gujarat, Kathiawar and parts of Rajasthan there existed another extensive development in a related architectural style. At Girnar, Palitana and Taranga, the Jain temple cities and places of pilgrimage, there is much sculpture still in situ. The most remarkable examples of this style, however, are to be seen in Mount Abu, at the temples of Vimla Shah (AD 1032) and Tejahpala (AD 1232). These are domed shrines with pillared halls.[11]

After the invasion of Muslims during the thirteenth century

the Hindu rulers of the north were swept aside. Muslims captured almost all the principal cities of north and south India by the fourteenth century. In the resulting confusion new Hindu powers like the Vijaynagar Empire survived till 1565. The style of the Vijaynagar temples were rich and ornate. Around the temples simple open pavilions were erected. But after the defeat of the Hindu Kingdoms the Hindu Kings lost their spirit to build and became increasingly inward looking. The interiors of the temples were dark and gloomy and statues were made of dark materials, their grotesque shapes emphasized by the light from flickering oil lamps. Thus sculpture as an art form of expression began to dwindle and went into oblivion. After a long gap, in recent times, this form has begun to revive itself and reassert its native vitality and expressiveness.

From the foregoing discussion on sculpture as a source material for research, we find that there are significant clues and rich depictions of art forms, preserved in the sculptural heritage of India, which can be explored and would provide valuable insights for research in music and the performing arts.

PAINTING

The history of Indian Painting indicates that the mood of music, musical performances and musical instruments have been a favourite theme of painters, since time immemorial. During its long journey through history, painting has passed through several stages and has always maintained a profound continuity, consistency, and its own unique character.

As Dr. Karan Singh writes,

> From the very dawn of civilization the artistic urge in man has led him to produce works of abiding beauty and significance, often directly connected with his religious and spiritual strivings. Recent excavations have shown that even in pre-historic times cave dwellers used to embellish their primitive habitations with paintings which possess remarkable vigour and grace. It is clear that the artistic impulse is one of the most fundamental elements in the human psyche, and through the ages Man has expressed his hopes and aspirations, his dreams and innermost urges, through the medium of art. Indeed this essentially indefinable capacity to create and perceive beauty is one of the few distinguishing features between Man and the millions of other

species that inhabit this planet. The Indian artistic tradition is among the most ancient and richly varied in the history of mankind. A feature, particularly important in Indian art is that, unlike the great creations of ancient Greece or Egypt, Babylon or Mexico, it represents a tradition that is still alive and vibrant in the life of millions of human beings. This is the special fascination of India and the reason why Indian art is of much deeper than merely archival or historical interest.[12]

Literary works testify to the eminence of painting as an art form in India, particularly in the decoration of walls, but climate has taken a devastating toll, leaving behind only a few tantalizing examples. Although painting in India should have a history stretching as far back as any of the other arts, yet because of its perishable nature, little has survived. None of the examples found in rock shelters over almost all of India, and chiefly representing scenes of hunting and war, appears to be earlier than the eighth century BC, and all may be as late as the tenth century AD. A faint idea of painter's art can be had from the pottery, elaborately decorated with leaf designs and geometrical patterns.

In the classical Sanskrit literature, painting is considered an occupation not unworthy of princes. There are so many references to painted portraits in Sanskrit literature that evidently the prohibition in the *silpa-shastras* applied only to temples and other sacred buildings and not to the practice of painting as a secular accomplishment. In a play attributed to Kalidasa the heroine is Queen Dharini's beautiful attendant Malvika, who is a skilful musician and dancer. The Queen carefully keeps her attractive handmaid from the presence of the King, Agnimitra, but foolishly caused Malvika's portrait to be painted on the walls of the *chitra-sala*. The plot of the play discloses the disastrous consequences of the King's next visit to the picture gallery. Of this secular art of painting of the pre-Muhammadan times there are no Indian examples extant, but from what we know of the religious sculpture and of the technical excellence of the best paintings of the Ajanta School, we can fairly assume that the merit ascribed to it by Sanskrit writers was not overrated.[13]

The earliest substantial remains of Indian painting are those found in the rock-cut cave temples at Ajanta, in the western part of India. These belong to the second or first century BC, and are in a style reminiscent of the relief sculpture at Sanchi. At Ajanta some of the most substantial remains of Indian painting are of about the fifth century BC and a little later, when this ancient civilization was in full flower. The paintings decorate the walls and ceilings of the numerous cave temples. The themes illustrate the major events of the Buddha's life, and the Jataka tales. The ceilings are covered with rich motifs, based generally upon the lotus stem and the world of animals and birds.

Like the sculptures of the Gupta period, the Ajanta paintings created a norm, and bequeathed a style, that is expansive, free and dynamic, unlike anything seen in later Indian paintings. Out of the twenty-nine caves only six are important from the point of view of paintings. The six caves are numbers one, two, nine, ten, sixteen and seventeen. The narrative compositions in the paintings handled with utmost dexterity. Being the natural outgrowth of the long traditions of relief sculpture they reflect the splendour and maturity of contemporary sculpture. The large images of the Bodhisattvas in Cave I, combining rich elegance with spiritual serenity, reflect a vision that sees the shifting world of matter and the transcendental calm of Nirvana as essentially one.[14]

Except for a large and magnificent painting of a dance scene found at the rock cut cave at Bagh—a painting executed in a style closely resembling Ajanta—hardly any other work of this great period survives. The cave temples at Badami, in the Karnataka country, and Sittanavasal, in Tamil Nadu, probably of the late sixth and seventh centuries AD are only echoes of the style of the fifth century, which appears to have died out around this time.

The Ajanta style of painting was replaced in western India by what has been appropriately named as the Western Indian Style. Among the earliest examples are a few surviving wall paintings of the Kailash Temple (mid-eighth century), at Ellora and the Jain temples, built at the same site a hundred years later. The plastic sense of form, so evident at Ajanta, was emphatically replaced by a style that even at this early stage is heavily dependent on line. According to Havell,

> The decline of the wall painting was followed by the growth of styles of painting more often confined to book illustration, namely, the Pala School, of Bengal and Bihar, and the Western Indian school. The Pala

School, which came to an end about the late twelfth century, preserved the traditions of Ajanta to a greater extent, though these were cramped and confined within the small painting space available, and lack of sweeping freedom afforded by the large wall spaces of Ajanta. The paintings consist mainly of illustrations to Mahayana Buddhist texts and are iconographic in character. The colours employed are few, and we get a somewhat slavish imitation of the mannerisms of Ajanta art. The Western Indian style was also extraordinarily conservative, sticking with great tenacity to these characteristics for a period of over 500 years, almost to the end of the sixteenth century, though certain stylistic variations and elaborations are to be noticed in the various phases.[15]

Interestingly, most of the best examples of this style have survived not on the walls of temples, but in a large number of illustrated manuscripts commissioned by members of the Jaina community. The majority of the manuscripts are Jain Scriptures, but there is one secular example, that of Vasanta Vilas, dated 1457. Although the colouring is brilliant, the style is really one of pure draftmanship. The outline establishes all the facts and though it is very facile and almost careless, is extremely accomplished.

In Gujarat, Rajputana and Bundelkhand, as in most other parts of India, the ruling dynasties of the medieval period were mainly concerned with decorating temples and civic architecture with numerous sculptures and designs. For instance, the splendid Solanki temples of Gujarat and the famous Chandella temples of Khajuraho were not painted. Undoubtedly their builders appreciated the fact that it would be futile from the aesthetic point of view, to cramp the somewhat small interiors of beautifully carved stone temples by covering the limited wall space with a series of paintings executed by artistes whose inspiration was at a standstill.[16]

The Frescoes

The art or technique of painting moist plaster surface, by mixing of colours in lime water, is known as fresco painting. These were done with fingers or thin sticks. In this style walls dampened with water and coated with lime provided a surface on which designs were painted in different colours. The earliest known examples of frescoes are found at the world famous monastery of the Ajanta caves, numbers 9 and 10. Said to belong to the first century BC or the early part of the first century, these frescoes are a product of the Andhra School, which began with the sculptures of Bhaja in the first century BC and ended with the last reliefs of Amravati and Nagarjunakonda in the third century AD. The inspiration of these early frescoes, as well as the later work of Ajanta, was derived from Buddhism. The late sixth century AD Chalukyan frescoes of Badami and the early seventh century AD Pallava frescoes of Sittanavasal are more or less in the tradition of the last phase of Ajanta. The tradition of wall painting continued in south India even in the eighth and ninth centuries AD as evidenced by the frescoes of Kanchipuram, Tirumalaipuram and the remnants of the early frescoes in the erstwhile Travancore state.[17] Frescoes were also done in the style used in the Jain temples; and decorate the walls and ceilings of numerous cave temples and monasteries at the site. They are executed in the tempera or frescoe technique on smooth surfaces, prepared by application of plaster.

The above-mentioned frescoes are mostly on themes such as the life of the Buddha, the Jataka tales, etc. But evidently from the point of view of the scholars of music these frescoes are very valuable works, because of the information that can be gathered from them on musical instruments, dance, costume, orchestra of that period.

Palm Leaf Paintings

Paintings on palm leaves, belonging to ancient India, were in vogue for a very long period (from the first to the eighth century). Small illustrations on palm leaf, chiefly painted at the great Buddhist establishments of eastern India, appear to have conserved some elements of the ancient style. In the words of Khandalvala,

> The art of wall painting, taken as a whole, appears to have degenerated from the tenth century AD onwards. While it was in this neglected condition an interesting development took place, almost simultaneously, in two widely distant parts of the country. This development consisted of (a) the production in Gujarat of illustrated manuscripts on palm leaf of Jain canonical works, and (b) the production in Bengal

and Bihar of illustrated Buddhist manuscripts on palm leaf during the rule of Pala kings. The ancestry of both the Gujarati and Pala manuscript illustrations is to be traced to medieval wall paintings such as those of the ninth century AD at Ellora. The early Gujarati manuscript illustrations, as also the Pala manuscript illustrations, are on palm leaf in Gujarat and also in Nepal where the Pala style continued to flourish after its extinction in Bengal.[18]

Gradually, as palm leaf was replaced by paper as a carrier of information during the fourteenth and fifteenth centuries, and with its ever-increasing use landscape elements were frequently introduced into the composition and a sense of pictorial narration was developed.

Mughal Miniature Paintings

After the establishment of Muslim rule in India the art of painting took a new turn, which may be described as the true integrated style of painting, a combination of two cultures: the ancient Indian and Persian. It began with Humayun who requisitioned the services of two famous painters, Mir Sayyad Ali and Khwaja Abdus Samad, from Persia to illustrate the *Hamza Namah*, a collection of 360 tales about Amir Hamza, a legendary hero of early Islam. The early Mughals were greatly under the influence of Persian culture and they introduced the art of miniature painting at their courts with the aid of Persian artists. But the accession of numerous Indian painters, trained under the Persian masters, to the Mughal atelier, and the growth of a more original outlook, which favoured Indian types, scenes, and realistic, sensitive portraiture, resulted in a school of miniature painting with marked characteristics of its own. By AD 1585 the Mughal school had shed its early Indo-Persian character and was developing on original lines of its own.[19] In the opinion of Gluk,

> The fact that all these elements are recognisable in one and the same picture in association not quite unified, shows that our pictures belong to an initial stage of true Moghul art, in which the Persian factor which came in with Humayun still predominates, but in which the native Indian factor later brought in by Akbar is already apparent; and where an independent court life has become vigorous enough to borrow and incorporate foreign formulae of even more distant origin without

being subservient to them. (Abstract from the quotation in A.K. Coomaraswamy's *Introduction to Indian Art*, by Mulk Raj Anand, p. 88.)

Encouragement from Akbar and Shahjahan helped the art of Mughal miniature painting attain a high level of excellence. Jahangir displayed his love for art amply both in life and writing. The art and artists developed a great deal under the patronage of the emperor. Ustad Mansur, Manohar and Abul Hasan were among his artists. During this period portrait painting also flourished to a great extent. Consequently, a Rajasthan School of miniature developed, which was influenced by the Mughal style. As Guha has rightly stated the Mughal miniature and Rajput miniature are two monads, each strictly circumscribed and complete within itself, yet acting upon one another. The very conception of miniature painting is the contribution of Islamic court art, and Rajasthani miniature was closely affiliated to Mughal miniature. It appears, therefore, that Hindu art tradition going round and round in a circle made sudden sally en route and reappeared among fresh woods and new pastures.[20]

According to some authors the calligraphic style left its mark on the character of most Mughal paintings. Indian connoisseurs of this art distinguish the various styles of draughtsmanship which developed in different localities or families of painters by the term 'Kalam' (pen) or brush. The lines were drawn with a fine brush usually made from the hair of a squirrel's tail.

A preliminary outline sketch was made in Indian red, used without gum, so that when dry, the colour could be brushed away, leaving a very faint indication of the drawing. The finished line was then drawn with lampblack specially prepared by burning a camphorated cotton wick in a mustard-oil lamp. Sometimes the drawing was delicately shaded, and some of the detail heightened with gold or tinted. The artists prided themselves on the fineness of their brushes, and the test of supreme skill was to finish the detail with an 'ek balkalam', a one haired brush, which seems to have been used for microscopic stippling as well as for the finest lines.[21]

Rajput miniature painting developed between the sixteenth and nineteenth centuries in the work of artists attached to the courts of Rajput princes. Geographically, it may be divided into a number of local schools in Rajputana, the Deccan, the Punjab, the Himalayas and Garhwal. The themes painted by the artists include Raginis, the personifications of musical modes connected with phases of love, illustrations of Indian epics and romantic legend of gods Vishnu and Krishna. Rajput painting is a combination of folk art and hierarchic classic traditions and more often than a reduction of the themes and techniques of mural painting to the intimate scale. Whereas the early miniature of Rajasthan is primitive in conceptual presentation and decorative pattern, some of the later paintings, like the eighteenth century illuminations of the Kangra school in the Punjab, display a sophisticated combination of realism and lyric grace. Invariably, as in monumental painting, sacred legend is presented as contemporary experience. Although early Mughal painting was an outgrowth of the Persian miniature style, in the great period under emperors Jahangir and Shahjahan the artists produced illuminations of extraordinarily realistic character, perhaps under European influence blended with elements of Persian and Indian origin. In Mughal painting it is possible to differentiate between the works of local schools in Delhi, Lucknow, Jaipur, etc. The themes of the Mughal artists included events from the court, portraits and occasional subjects drawn from the world of the Hindu epics.[22]

Ragamala Paintings

As we know, for classifying the Raagas in Indian music, the Raag Raagini system was evolved during the seventeenth, eighteenth and nineteenth centuries. There were said to be four Mats (schools) during that period: (1) Kallinath Mat (2) Somesvar Mat (3) Hanuman Mat and (4) Bharat Mat. The painters of this period innovated a unique style of painting in which the raagas of the Raag Raagini classification system became the objects of the painting. These Raagas were pictorially visualized in Indian miniatures, and came to be known as Ragamala Paintings. During the three centuries, sixteenth to the nineteenth, thousands of Ragamala Paintings were created by various schools in distinct styles. These paintings were arranged in albums containing most often thirty-six or forty-two folios, under a system of 'families'. Each family headed by a (male) Raaga included five or six Raaginis (wives). Sometimes it also included several Ragputras (sons), even Ragputris (daughters) and wives of sons. The paintings mostly portray romantic or devotional situations in a somewhat stereotyped, artistocratic setting. Only a small number of such paintings are actually dated and signed. Most can be placed with a high degree of certainty, into particular periods and the origins of others are disputed (Klaus, 1973: 14).

All known surviving examples of this art were painted in the sixteenth through nineteenth centuries in Rajasthan, central India, Deccan, the Ganges-Yamuna plains, or in the Pahari region. According to Claus Ebeling:

> Ragamala Painting appears to stand at a crossroad of Indian music, poetry, and miniature painting. It labels its individual paintings with the names of musical modes; it gathers the single pages into Ragamala albums, which are arranged in an order similar to the 'Garland of Raagas' of ancient and medieval authorities of musical learning. These garlands of Raagas were devices of memorization and classification for the musician who associated the individual modes with deities to whom the Raagas were dedicated. Poets then intrigued with this deification of Raagas, spun elaborate situations around their characters. In fact, the poetic versions conjure up images that often have a more human than divine quality or combine both in a fashion typical of many religious concepts in India. Both the musical and the poetic beginnings of Ragamalas are many centuries older than the painted versions. The introduction of paper and a blooming of miniature paintings in many parts of India, among Jains, Hindus and Muslims alike, brought with it the first illustrations of Ragamala poems or prayer formulas, probably between 1450 and 1550. A growing demand for copies of them, in the prevailing local fashion, developed during the next three hundred years.[23]

Among the many musical texts and poetic Ragamalas written in the distant past, a collection of verses by Meskarna, a court priest from Rewa, has had an important influence on the origin of the Ragamala painting. And this view is based on the surviving examples of the art. His work entitled 'Ragamala' still exists in four manuscripts, and bears a date that is equivalent to AD 1570. Establishing a sequential order it describes 6 Raagas, 31 Raaginis and 49 Putras in two series of verses. In the first series, verses 12-97, each musical mode is described as a personality. The second series, verses 98-109, compares the music of each mode to a sound in nature or in the household. Meskarna's system was used by the painters of Kulu, Basohli, Bilaspur, Garhwal and Kangra as their exclusive system for Ragamala. These schools are collectively known under the name Pahari.[24]

The Rajasthani style developed various schools of painting, whose Ragamala paintings were popular. And these included the schools of Mewar, Bundi, Kotah, Marwar, Bikaner, Kishangarh and Jaipur. It also had centres in Gujarat, Malwa, and Bundelkhand.

Mewar School

The Mewar School is among the most important schools of Ragamala painting. The earliest dated examples are represented by a Ragamala series painted at Chawand in 1605. These simple paintings, filled with bright colours, are only a step removed from the pre-Rajasthani phase. The style became more elaborate by the first quarter of the seventeenth century when another Ragamala series was painted in Udaipur in 1628 (formerly in the Khajanchi Collection, Bikaner, now dispersed in various collections).[25] Historians mention the names of Naseeruddin and Sahibdin as the famous painters of this style during the period.

Bundi and Kotah Style

Another important school of this art developed at Bundi and later at Kotah. The earliest examples are represented by a Ragamala series of extraordinarily rich quality, probably dating from the end of the sixteenth century. From the very beginning the Bundi style seemed to have found Mughal painting an inspiring source, but its workmanship was as distinctively Rajasthani as the work of Mewar. The output of miniature paintings towards the second-half of the seventeenth century indicates that this was a period of prolific activity. Simultaneously, Kotah also became an important centre of painting. The Ragamalas of the Kotah School became popular for its workmanship and style, and for maintaining until the very end its integrity despite the rapidly increasing Western influence.

Malwa Style

In the Malwa region, the Ragamala miniatures are quite archaistic, with mannerisms inherited from the sixteenth century retained until the end of the seventeenth century.[26] The arts and letters, lore and customs of Malwa were influenced by neighbouring Rajputana, the Jains of Gujarat, and Muslim culture of the Sultanates of Gujarat, the Deccan and Jaunpur. Ruled by Muslim Turks from 1436 to 1531, and by Pathans from 1535 to 1560, Mandu went through two styles of painting. Under the name Rajgarh, a unified Rajput state grew prosperous, numerous Ragamalas with a scroll band decorating the bottom of each painting, still belong to the united state of Rajgarh.[27]

Marwar Style

A Ragamala series dated 1623 reveals that painting in this state shared features common to other schools of Rajasthan. A very large amount of work was done in the Marwar style in the nineteenth century, all of which was highly stylized but strong in colour and often of great charm.

Bikaner Style

Of all the Rajasthani schools of painting, the Bikaner style, from its very inception in the mid-seventeenth century, shows the greatest indebtedness to the Mughal style. Delicacy of line and colour are consistent characteristics of Bikaner towards the end of the eighteenth century.[28] At the end of the seventeenth century Sirohi (Mount Abu) produced a small number of Ragamalas of a beautiful and unique style.

Jaipur (Amber) Style

Although the rulers were closely allied to the Mughal dynasty, the Jaipur style paintings of the sixteenth and early seventeenth centuries possessed all of the elements of the Rajasthani style. Of the Rajasthani styles of this period, the Jaipur school was the most popular, examples of which have been found all over northern India. The first Ragamala to be ascribed to Amber may have been painted during the time of Raja Man Singh. The badly damaged surviving pages of these paintings are now in the Baroda Museum. The only dated Ragamala of the Amber tradition is the one which was finished in 1709 at Amber Fort. Although it is possible that all Amber Ragamalas are products of the early eighteenth century, there is room for the theory that this iconographic tradition indeed started in the mid-seventeenth century. During the reign of Sawai Jai Singh II (1699-1743), the founder of Jaipur, another Ragamala style came into vogue probably in Jaipur. And was based on the Rajasthani tradition. A third style of Ragamalas flourished for several decades at the beginning of the nineteenth century in Jaipur and other places, starting probably in the reign of Pratap Singh known for his interest in music and painting.[29]

Pahari Style (Basohli and Kangra)

The Pahari style can be divided into two main schools, Basohli and Kangra. Unlike Rajasthan, these schools were not confined to the centres after which they are named, but extended all over the area. The earliest dated paintings are illustrations to the *Rasmanjari* of Bhanudatta (a Sanskrit work of poetics) belonging to the Basohli style. Stylistic comparsions have placed the earliest Pahari Ragamalas into the following decades. The Basohli style faded by the mid-eighteenth century, being gradually replaced by the Kangra Style, named after the state of Kangra. A curvilinear line, easy flowing rhythms, calmer colours, and a mood of sweet lyricism easily distinguish the work from that of the Basohli style. The reasons of this change are to be sought in strong influences from the plains, notably the Mughal styles of Delhi and Lucknow. The finest work of this style was produced largely around AD 1775-1820.[30]

Claus Ebeling offers interesting observations on the note-worthy aspects of the Ragamala paintings which opens up several paths for the researchers in the field of music to think about. According to him Vasant Vilasa is a poem, produced in Ahmedabad and dated AD 1451, that contains numerous paintings which conspicuously match the later Ragamala iconogrpahics. The verses of this work abound with verbal imagery which is closely related to that of the Ragamala paintings, and poetry. He further states that Nayikabheda and Krishnalila, as it occurs in the Ragamala painting, is by no means an unrelated phenomenon. And that in *Rasikpriya's* Hindi translation, its author Keshav Das discussed the proper poetic treatment of Nayikas and Nayaks based on the example of romance of Radha and Krishna. In a similar fashion and at the same time, Ragamala painting incorporated elements of this romance into the encounters of Raagas and Raaginis, giving them the identities of Radha and Krishna. In short, he points out that the three main roots of Ragamala painting grew out of music, Ragmala poetry and painting in general. Basically, music contributed the concept of 'Garland of Raagas'; the names of Raagas; some Rasas, the emotional flavours; some performance times; and dhyanas, prayer formulas, which personify the melody. Ragamala poetry, based on the older dhyanas, provided the iconographics which were ultimately used in Ragamala painting. General miniature painting supplied the regional painterly styles and techniques.[31]

Modern Style of Painting

Towards the late nineteenth century, traditional Indian painting started dying out rapidly and was replaced by feeble works in a variety of idioms, all strongly influenced by the West. In the twentieth century a reaction against Western mannerisms took place, especially in Bengal, where a considerable number of works were produced in the modern style. The glory of Indian art was rediscovered, and the school consciously tried to produce what it considered to be a truly Indian art. Its leading artists were Rabindranath Tagore, and Abanindranath Tagore, and the theoretician E.B. Havell, the principal of the Calcutta School of Art. Amrita Sher-Gil, an important artist of modern Indian painting, made painters aware of new traditions, and directions. Modern day Indian painting is very much a part of the Indian scene.

The examination of the various styles of Indian painting reveals that music related subjects have been one of the major themes in Indian paintings from the earliest times. These paintings provide interesting clues to the types of musical instruments used by musicians in the earlier times, which can be an important source for research in the evolution and development of musical instruments in India. Further, the paintings also provide evidence of different forms of group orchestrations as well as solo performances. These paintings also reflect the place of music in the society in spheres, such as in temples, on religious and sacred occasions, imperial courts, processions, and social events.

The most significant aspect of Indian painting in its relationship to music, however, is the Ragamala style. In which the different raagas, their philosophy of raag dhyan and mood, the manifestations of the time theory of music, and the feelings sought to be expressed through a particular raaga are vividly picturized through the characters, colours, and setting chosen by the artist. This unique characteristic of the Ragamala paintings raises the raagas to their highest forms of aesthetic expression.

Thus the Indian painting traditions provide a rich and insightful source for research in music.

Manuscripts

Manuscripts refer to the original handwritten documents and other materials recorded on paper, palm leaves, birch bark, wooden, metallic and other surfaces that are primary sources of information for any type of historical research. Manuscripts are a vital source of information in the field of research in music, especially in the study of its historical aspects and development of theory and practice at different places and times. It is noteworthy that the treasure of wisdom and thoughts preserved in our Shastrik texts like the *Natyashastra, Brihaddeshi* and *Sangeet Ratnakar,* etc., is the major source of knowledge and information for research in Indian musicology, which came through original manuscripts.

Manuscripts are the carriers of culture in society, therefore, all possible efforts should be made to preserve them. Even if printed versions of manuscripts are available, it is essential to preserve them as a token of gratitude to our forefathers, who had made the effort to pass down the light of knowledge. Manuscripts are also useful in tracing the history of scripts. Hence there is an obligation to preserve them intact for posterity.

Prof. M.V. Sitaramaiah touchingly drives home the need for preserving a manuscript along with its microfilm copy. He very aptly asks: 'Is it not like ignoring an ailing father after taking his photograph, if a manuscript is neglected just because it has been microfilmed?'[32]

V. Raghavan quotes a Sanskrit verse on the preservation of manuscripts, its translation into English is as follows:

> The manuscript should be dressed as one's good offspring is dressed, be guarded from mishandling of others like a textile land, be thoroughly learned everyday like a wounded limb, be visited (i.e. handled) everyday like a dear friend, be bound fast with a strong thread like a prisoner, be remembered always like the name of the Lord; such a book gets never deteriorated. So say the masters.[33]

The traditional method of preserving texts of damaged manuscripts was copying them manually. A process not only laborious and time consuming, but in which errors were inevitable. In modern times, there are mechanical devices that help in preserving the facsimile of the manuscripts.

Currently foremost among such devices is the microfilming of manuscripts. In addition to being extremely handy in preserving manuscripts in their original handwriting, the microfilm occupies less space than its hard copy and is easy to store and maintain. However, the original manuscripts should be preserved as part of the national heritage. Microfiche and xerography are the other two devices used for storing texts of manuscripts. Paper manuscripts have an advantage over the palm leaf manuscripts as their copies can be reproduced xerographically (xerox). Not only is xeroxing economical, since it is printed on paper it can be read in the ordinary way without the help of a machine. Whereas manuscripts stored on microfilm, microfiche/microcard need a microfilm/microfiche reader. Microfiche is also printed on a card, hence called microcard, and needs an opaque reader.

The Indira Gandhi National Centre for the Arts, New Delhi, under its Kalanidhi programme, which includes a national library of microfilms and microfische of all manuscripts, has been catering to the needs of scholars and students. Recently, the Ford Foundation offered a grant including provision for equipment, to microfilm the manuscripts in the Oriental

Research Institute, Mysore. It may be noted here that Japan has a unique traditional system of preserving ancient paintings. The method is laborious, and calls for utmost patience. Even the preparation of the glue involves a complex process in which the special ingredients have to be reduced to very fine paste in a stone mortar, boiled and kept in jars to be used 12 years later.[33] The Library system of the University of Delhi is also doing a commendable job of maintaining a large manuscript section. Many valuable manuscripts in the field of music are preserved in the Rampur Raza Library, Rampur in Uttar Pradesh and the Khuda Baksh Oriental Public Library, Patna in Bihar.

Oral Tradition

The unbroken link of continuity which binds our musical tradition with the tradition propounded by Bharata, the earliest extant authority on music, is mainly maintained by the traditional *moukhik parampara* (the oral tradition). India has given to the world the knowledge and wisdom of the highest order through the Vedas. It has placed Indian culture on a solid foundation which can spread the message for centuries to come. Even after thousands of years the Vedas are still relevant today. The knowledge of the Vedas, intact in its purity and form, was passed down the ages through the oral tradition, the oldest tradition in the world. In this system the *guru* teaches the *shishya* in a highly disciplined atmosphere. The training imparted in such a system is not only individualistic, but also scientific. And that is the reason why the *Sutras* from Vedas are recited with the highest precision, pitch, rhythm and tonal modulation, even today. Although in ancient times there were no electronic devices to preserve the system, it is the oral tradition, which kept it alive. In this system the words uttered by teachers are regarded as '*Ved vakya*' and the disciple is supposed to learn them wholeheartedly with the fullest devotion.

The system of oral tradition still exists in the field of performing arts. The oral system of teaching has a great significance in these fields. For example, in the rendering of Raaga 'Bhairav' or Raaga 'Shree', the use of Komal Rishabh has a special place, but its implication and application in both the Raagas, and the manner in which it should be practised, can only be taught by the *guru* or teacher orally. Similarly, there are three different types of sounds produced through distinct parts of the human body, i.e. navel, heart, throat, and from the nasal area. This is a specialized knowledge imparted by the *guru* to the *shishya* demonstrating the technique of producing sounds from different parts of the body. There is no other way of imparting this knowledge except through the oral tradition.

Music being a practice oriented discipline, there are certain elements of learning and knowledge that cannot be transmitted through writing. This is the principal reason that a strong oral tradition has sustained and preserved the originality, and maintained the continuity of form and styles of music over the centuries. A great deal of knowledge and insights about such tradition is not, and to some extent cannot, be transmitted through writing. Therefore, research in music, unlike social sciences, requires awareness of the richness of the oral tradition as a source of information. A researcher who wishes to study the various practice related aspects of music will have to obtain information mainly through the oral tradition. For this purpose it would be necessary to develop a close rapport and interaction with the maestros to obtain the required information, insights, and knowledge on the subject.

A rich resource of data collection for research in Indian music is the collection of recorded music in various archives, such as the All India Radio, and music and research academies in the various parts of India. In these archives the recordings of performances by the old masters and well known contemporary musicians belonging to various *gharanas* are being preserved and made available to researchers. These collections are extraordinarily helpful to researchers as they enable a close, critical, and comparative study of the various *gharanas*, and also help recognize the creative styles and modifications developed by the artists. The information available in these archives is important not only for studying the styles of musicians of different schools, but is also an extremely important and authentic source for examining other aspects of music in which researches are being carried out at present. In this connection special mention may be made of the Research Academy, Calcutta, and the Sangeet Natak Akademi, New Delhi, where considerable dedicated efforts are being made to preserve the heritage of Indian music.

With the advancement of technology, greater use is being made of the electronic media for audiovisual recordings of musical performances. The use of computer is also becoming quite common in the various archives, which will facilitate access to the collections and data stored at different places. The use of the Internet and the World Wide Web makes it possible to obtain information about sources of data in libraries and archives all over the world. This new development in communication is of considerable importance for research in music and is discussed in the next chapter.

NOTES

1. W. Ro-esijadi, *The Buddhist Inspiration, Sculpture*, Newsweek Books, New York, 1975, p. 41.
2. J.P. Guha, *Introducing Indian Art*, R. and K. Publishing House, New Delhi, 1963, p. 102.
3. *The Last Two Million Years*, edited by the Reader's Digest Association, London, 1974, p. 161.
4. E.B. Havell, *The Art Heritage of India*, D.B. Taraporevala Sons and Co. Pvt. Ltd., Bombay, 1964, p. 32.
5. Ibid., p. 41.
6. W. Ro-esijadi, op. cit., p. 44.
7. J.P. Guha, op. cit., pp. 126-8.
8. *The Last Two Million Years*, op. cit., p. 163.
9. J.P. Guha, op. cit., p. 61.
10. Ibid., p. 54.
11. *Indian Art, Encyclopaedia Britannica*, Vol. 12, 1964, p. 230 B.
12. K. Singh, 'Foreword', in C. Ebeling, *Ragamala Painting*, R. Kumar Gallery, New Delhi, 1973.
13. E.B. Havell, op. cit., p. 67.
14. *Encyclopaedia Britannica* (Micropaedia), Vol. 27.
15. E.B. Havell, op. cit., p. 69.
16. Karl Khandalavala, *Brief Survey of Indian Painting*, New Book Co., Bombay, 1958, p.1.
17. Ibid., pp. 1-2
18. Ibid., pp. 3-4
19. Ibid., p. 6
20. Guha, op. cit., p. 152.
21. See, Moti Chandra, *Technique of Mughal Painting*, Lucknow, 1949.
22. *Encyclopaedia Britannica*, op. cit., p. 230 B.

23. C. Ebeling, *Ragamala Painting*, R. Kumar Gallery, New Delhi, 1973, p. 14.
24. Ibid., p. 64.
25. *Encyclopaedia Britannica* (Macropaedia), Vol. 27, South Asian Arts, p. 789.
26. Ibid., p. 790.
27. C. Ebeling, op. cit., pp. 39-40.
28. *Encyclopaedia Britannica,* op. cit., p. 790.
29. See C. Ebeling, op. cit., p. 42.
30. Ibid., p. 791.
31. Ibid., pp. 46-50.
32. R.S.S. Murthy, *Introduction to Manuscriptology*, Sharda Publishing House, Delhi, 1996, p. 77.
33. R.S.S. Murthy, op. cit., pp. 88-91.

CHAPTER 9

Research on the Internet

Since the Internet has become an important source of information for researchers and scholars worldwide, it is increasingly being consulted as a repository for research activity. Clearly, the Internet has created an environment ripe for a revolution which will transform society in the coming decades. Computers have already changed the lives of scholars and researchers from all fields of knowledge. E-mail has transformed scientific communication and electronic databases have expanded access to information. Unlike the past, when the traditional resource for information seekers was the public library, researchers of today are truly living in the age of information.

Using the Internet can be very exciting as there is something new each time it is accessed. An important strength of this communication tool is the fact that the people using it are from diverse backgrounds and there is no central control on it. Also, the medium has a two-way access. Information can be received as well as sent out on the Internet.

The Internet

The Internet is a collection of tens of thousands of computer networks that exchange information according to some agreed-upon, uniform rules or protocols.[1] On the Internet, a user has access to a wide variety of services: electronic mail, file transfer, vast information resources, interest group membership, interactive collaboration, multimedia displays, and more. The Internet can be a substantive source of academic information. It also provides a useful means for researchers to communicate with each other, through electronic mail and discussion groups. In addition to information on a large number of topics, the Internet provides contact with other researchers, databases of reference material and places where one can discuss topics, and seek help.

In one sense the Internet is no different from other information sources. Some information is free, some has to be paid for. Some information is of high quality and highly relevant to the research problem in hand. Others are of low quality and irrelevant. One popular misconception about the Internet is that it is a source of free information about everything. Much of the information on the Internet which is of value for academic research has to be paid for, and often doesn't come cheap. A researcher must always remember that there is a lot of information which is not available on the Internet. The amount of material available in print continues to increase every year. In general, academic research which has been commercially published is not freely available on the Internet. Some material may be made available through subscriptions to online versions of academic journals.

The Internet is a medium in which individuals can publish with minimum a small amount of technical skills, and access to a host computer. This is an important fact to remember while locating sites in the course of research. Internet sites change over time according to the commitment and inclination of the creator. Some sites demonstrate an expert's knowledge, while others are amateur efforts.

Types of Information Sources Available

One of the most popular and effective ways to tap into its resources is through the World Wide Web which is a vast collection of information on the Internet connected like a web. It has no beginning or end; the information is accessible in a non-linear fashion through connections called hyperlinks.[2] A number of different types of information sources are available on the World Wide Web. These include:

(i) Search engines, which are tools that provide keyword searching capability. An Internet search engine allows the user to enter keywords relating to a topic and retrieve information about Internet sites containing those keywords. Search engines are available for many of the Internet protocols.

Search engines located on the World Wide Web have become quite popular. Web search engines have the advantage of offering access to a vast range of information resources located on the Internet.

With most search engines, you fill out a form with your search terms and then ask that the search proceed. The engine searches its index and generates a page with links to those resources containing some or all of your terms. These resources are usually presented in a relevancy ranked order. A new development in search engine technology is the ordering of search results by concept, keyword, site, links or popularity. Engines that support these features may be thought of as second generation search engines. All search engines have rules for formulating queries. It is imperative that you read the help files at the site before proceeding. Online tutorials can also help you learn the rules.

(ii) Meta-search tools, which allow you to access databases from one place.

(iii) Subject directories of a general collection of Internet and WWW resources. An increasing number of universities, libraries, companies, organizations, and even volunteers are creating subject directories to catalogue portions of the Internet. These directories are organized by subject and consist of links to Internet resources relating to these subjects. The major subject directories available on the Web tend to have overlapping but different databases. Most directories provide a search capability that allows you to query the database on your topic of interest.

There are two basic types of directories: academic and professional directories often created and maintained by subject experts to support the needs of researchers, and commercial portals that cater to the general public and are competing for traffic.

(iv) Virtual libraries, which are directories or subject catalogues consisting of selected Web resources.

(v) Specialized databases which contain comprehensive collections of hyperlinks in a particular subject area, or are self-contained, searchable indexes made available on the Web.

(vi) Library catalogue accessible on the World Wide Web.

(vii) FTP archives, which are collections of files in various formats available on the Internet.

(viii) E-mail discussion groups, of which several thousand groups exist to share opinions and experiences, ask and answer questions, or post and answer questions, or post information about a specific topic. E-mail discussion groups tend to be associated with academic institutions. Many topics are scholarly in nature, and it is not unusual for experts in the field to be among the participants.

(ix) Usenet newsgroups, which are collections of group discussions, questions and answers, and other information that have been shared through the Internet.

Evaluation of Information on the Internet

Theoretically, anyone who wants to should be able to cruise the information superhighway. Therefore, one presumes that finding and interpreting the vast amounts of information available would be an easy task to accomplish. However, in practice it is very different.

The traditional resource for researchers has been the reference desk of libraries. Here too, there are vast amounts of information to navigate, but the reference desk generally contains a librarian to act as a guide. The Internet with its almost infinite resources, would seem to be an ideal reference tool. However, the vast amount of information that makes it such an attraction for researchers, makes it unwieldy and difficult to navigate. The researchers need to understand different category-based searching and sophisticated search techniques.

The quality of information also needs to be critically assessed by the researcher. Print sources that are available through a research or academic library have often been put through a screening process by professional librarians. There are several virtual libraries on the Internet, but for research purposes it would be useful to consult those in which information is evaluated before it is listed.

Since it is relatively easy to publish information on the Internet, one needs to be absolutely sure that the information being used for research purposes is authentic and reliable. As a result, full investigation should be done on questions like (i) who is the author or institution, (ii) how current is the information, (iii) who is the audience, (iv) what is the purpose of the information.

In order to answer the above questions, one can look for the name of the author or institution at the top or bottom of a Web page. Going to the home page of the site hosting the information to find out about the organization can also help. A search engine can also be used to see what related information is available on the Web. Usually, web sites give an E-mail address for contact. The researcher can write at this address to further confirm the source of information on the site. Most often, Web pages have the date on which the information was last modified or updated. Researchers can check this to see how current the information is. In addition, there are a number of good resources, extensive guides and bibliographies on the Internet to help in evaluating available information.

The researcher also needs to evaluate the accuracy of the information available on the web. The information presented cannot be taken at its face value. One must remember that Web sites are rarely referred or reviewed, as scholarly journals and books are. The source of information on the Web site should clearly state whether it is original or borrowed from elsewhere. The researcher needs to use additional print and electronic sources to compliment the information provided.

Security and Legal Issues

When information is transmitted on the Internet, the communication that is sent passes through several different systems. It may take different routes to arrive at a destination. This opens the possibility of interception and examination of E-mail or other transmissions. Therefore, researchers need to use encryption techniques so that only the recipient of an E-mail for whom the information is meant can read it. Some countries have adopted laws to ensure privacy of electronic communications.

There are also issues of copyright on the Internet. It is difficult and time consuming to produce unauthorized copies of printed material due to its physical form. As information transmitted on the Internet is very easy to copy and store. A different set of laws are required to protect its copyright. In most cases, the information available on the Internet is the intellectual property of an individual or an organization and is protected by copyright laws. While gathering information, one must check to see if there are any copyright notices or information. Intellectual property rights are often violated as there are hardly any methods to check or prevent people from making copies of information available in the electronic form.

Issues Related to Effective use of the Internet for Research

The magnitude of information available on the Internet can entangle the unwary researcher. Also, the information must be used responsibly and cautiously. The following points need to be considered before researchers use this medium as an information resource:

(i) There is a significant learning curve before one can effectively use the Internet for research purposes. The researcher needs to learn efficient utilization of a variety of search tools and extract quality research information.
(ii) Online research requires different research techniques when compared to physical search. When extracting data from physical resources, the researcher needs to look up the card catalogue and other indexes to extract the specific information required. The Internet requires more sophisticated search techniques which involve use of search engines, directories, etc.
(iii) Much material on the Internet lacks the depth of a good encyclopaedia.
(iv) In order to use the Internet the researcher needs to have access to a computer and also the necessary time required to go online and search the information.

There is no doubt that the Internet is a powerful tool for research purposes. With a click of the 'mouse', one can have access to journal articles, reference materials, images, library and museum collections throughout the world. Besides, it provides access to the most current information. As a result the Internet has grown rapidly with millions of users worldwide and is being used extensively by researchers from all fields for information around the world.

NOTES

1. E. Ackermann and K. Hartman, *The Information Specialist's Guide to Searching on the Internet and the World Wide Web*, Fitzroy Dearborn Publishers, Chicago, 1999, p. 2.
2. Ibid., pp. 21-2.

CHAPTER 10

Synopsis: The Research Proposal

For starting any research study, the researcher needs to submit a formal proposal in the form of a synopsis of the research plan to the educational institution where the study is to be carried out, or to the sponsoring organization which may finance the research.

Synopsis is the formal document which contains the basic elements of a research plan. In other words, it is a gist of the proposed steps and components to be followed by the researcher giving an overview of the purpose and rationale of the study and the methods to achieve the desired results. Synopsis may be described as the research proposal which presents a problem, discusses related research activities, outlines the data needed for solving the problem, and indicates the design to be used to collect and analyse the data.

The research proposal is essentially a road map, indicating clearly the location from which the journey begins, the destination to be reached, and the method of getting there. Well prepared proposals include potential problems that may be encountered along the way and methods for avoiding or working around them much like a road map includes alternative routes in the case of a detour.[1] A research proposal in effect tells us: (1) What will be done? (2) Why it will be done? (3) How it will be done? (5) To whom it will be done? (6) What is the benefit of doing it?.[2]

The synopsis or a research proposal is helpful to the researcher as well as to the institution or organization sponsoring the research. For the researcher the process of writing down the thoughts relating to a proposed research study is extremely helpful in clarifying the research questions and focusing on the nature and scope of the study. The greater the attention and thought the researcher puts into the proposal, the easier it becomes for him/her to complete the research study. From the point of view of the institution, a research proposal is the first step in the evaluation process. It allows the sponsor to assess the sincerity of purpose of the researcher, the clarity of the design, the comprehensiveness of the background material, and competence of the researcher to undertake the project. It also helps the institution to assess the usefulness and relevance of the proposed research based upon the current institutional, scholastic, or scientific needs. Further, the research proposal provides the basis for a meaningful discussion and dialogue between the researcher and the sponsoring organization, or concerned research committee for the refinement of the topic and research design.

The development of a synopsis involves the following activities: a thorough analysis of the selected topic and formulation of the problem; review of literature and related researches; spell out the various steps for data collection and analysis; and cost and financial requirements of the project or plan to be incorporated, if required. All these elements of the proposed research study need to be written down in a concise form to help the institution or sponsoring organization in evaluating the proposal. The proposal is supposed to demonstrate the researcher's clarity of mind and ability to think logically, knowledge of the subject, discipline, and competence to carry out the research. The synopsis is beneficial for the researcher as it provides a tentative work plan that charts the logical steps needed to accomplish the stated goals.

A proposal is actually more beneficial for the novice researcher than for the sponsor. This does not diminish its relevance to the sponsor, but it is imperative for the beginner to have a tentative work plan that charts the logical steps needed to accomplish the stated goals. After the acceptance of the proposal, the document serves as a guide for the researcher throughout the investigation. Progress can be monitored and milestones noted. At the completion of the project, the proposal contains everything needed, outlining the final research report.[3]

The final benefit, especially for the novice researcher, is that the proposal forces time and budget estimates. These estimates allow the researcher to plan the project so that work progresses steadily towards the deadline. Since many people are inclined to procrastinate, having a schedule assists them in working methodically towards the completion of the project.

FORMAT FOR SYNOPSIS

The format for synopsis depends to a large extent on the nature of research and the requirements of the institution where research is to be carried out. However, there are certain common features that are found in almost all types of research proposals. The basic outline of the contents of a research proposal, keeping in view that proposals can be organized differently, is given below.[4]

1. Introduction
   A. The problem statement.
   B. A rationale for the research.

I. Statement of Research Objectives
   C. Hypothesis.
   D. Definition of terms.
   E. Summary including a restatement of the problem.
II. A (Brief) Review of the Relevant Literature.
   A. The importance of the question being asked.
   B. The current status of the topic.
   C. The relationship between literature and problem statement.
   D. Summary including a restatement of the relationships between the important variables under consideration and how these relationships are important to the hypothesis proposed in the introduction.
III. Method
   A. Participants including their description and selection procedures.
   B. Research design.
   C. Data Collection plans.
      1. Operational definition of all variables.
      2. Reliability and validity of instruments.
      3. Results of pilot studies.
   D. Proposed analysis of the data.
   E. Results of the data.
IV. Implications and Limitations
V. Appendices
   A. Copies of instruments that will be used.
   B. Results of pilot studies (actual data).

C. Human experimentation approval.
D. Participant permission form.
E. Time line.

As is evident from the above outline a research proposal is organized more or less in the same general sequence as chapter titles in any thesis or dissertation, i.e. introduction, review of literature, methodology, results and discussion. Since a research proposal cannot present an analysis of the limitations of the study, a quick guideline as to what a proposal should contain is provided in the first three sections of the finished proposal: introduction, review of the literature, and the method. The rest of the material should be included on the basis of the discussion between the researcher and the research guide.

Whereas the above stated format is more suitable for analytical researches, the format of synopsis in the fields of music and other performing arts and humanities is usually different. The research studies in these areas are mostly descriptive, either of type of case study or exploratory in nature. Therefore, the general structure of synopsis in these fields usually follows the pattern given below:

1. Introduction: A brief statement of the proposed topic and its importance.
2. Rationale of the study, stating the usefulness of the topic for the concerned subject.
3. Statement of objectives and scope of research, stating the period and region to be covered, etc.
4. A brief review of the historical background and the relevant literature.
5. A review of the current status of the topic and research studies already done on the subject or related areas.
6. Proposed methodology, research design; and a clear statement of hypotheses, if relevant.
7. Plan for data collection and proposed sample.
8. Proposed methods for analysis of data.
9. The nature of findings expected and their relevance for the advancement of knowledge in the field.
10. Implications and limitations of the proposed study.
11. Bibliography, of literature and other source material to be utilized.

12. Information about the sources of data collection, manuscripts, libraries, and other institutions to be contacted.
13. Appendices giving information about instruments and tests to be utilized for data collection, and copies of such instruments and tests, if available.

In most institutions of higher learning, where doctoral level research is conducted in the above stated areas, the synopsis is submitted in consultation with the research guide. Based on a discussion of the synopsis the research board or committee approves the proposed study. In this process the synopsis often gets revised and may even have to be rewritten several times. In most institutions the synopsis includes a chapter plan of the proposed thesis or dissertation. Such a plan gives a preview of the proposed thesis, as it would be written in the completed form. The chapter plan provides a useful framework to the researcher for completing the different parts of the thesis as he/she proceeds with the research work. The proposed chapters act as milestones for the progress and completion of the study. It may be noted here that as the research progresses many unanticipated problems and situations may arise that may lead to modifications in the research topic, methodology, or the scope of the study. The definition of the problem itself may undergo change as the researcher discovers more information on the subject. Similarly, the difficulties in data collection or findings from the field data may lead to changes in the direction and scope of the research. Consequently, it may become necessary to modify the topic in consultation with the research guide or supervisor, and the concerned research committee or board of research studies.

NOTES

1. C.W. Emory and D.R. Cooper, *Business Research Methods*, Richard D. Irwin, Homewood, Illinois, 1991, p. 112.
2. V.L. Lewis, and W.H. Baker, *Proposal Writing for the Data Processing Consultant*, Prentice Hall, Englewood Cliffs, New Jersey, 1986, p. 96.
3. Ibid., p. 51.
4. N.J. Salkind, *Exploring Research*, Prentice Hall, New Jersey, 1991, pp. 260-1.

Bibliography

Ackoff, Russel, L., *The Design of Social Research,* University of Chicago Press, Chicago, 1961.

Agarwal, V.S., *Heritage of Indian Art,* Publications Division, GOI, 1964.

Agrawal, R.A., *Marwar Murals,* Agam Kala Prakashan, New Delhi, 1977.

Aldred, Cyril, *The Development of Egyptian Art,* Tiranti Ltd., London, 1965.

Allen, T. Harrel, *New Methods in Social Science Research,* Praeger Publishers, New York, 1987.

Berdie, Douglas R. and John F. Anderson, *Questionnaires, Design and Use,* The Scarecrow Press, Inc., Metuchen, N.J., 1974.

Best, J.W., *Research in Education,* Prentice Hall, Englewood Cliffs, 1959.

Bingham, W.V. and B.V. Moore, *How to Interview,* Harper, N.Y., 1941.

Brijbhushan, Jamila, *The World of Indian Miniatures,* Kodansha International Ltd., Tokyo, 1979.

Bush, M.B., *Survey of Research in Education,* M.S. University, Baroda, 1974.

Clover, Vernon T. and L. Balsley Howard, *Business Research Methods,* Grid, Inc., Columbus, Ohio, 1974.

Cohen, Morris and Ernest Nagel, *An Introduction to Logic and Scientific Method,* Harcourt, Brace, New York, 1934.

Coomaraswami, A.K., *Catalogue of Indian Collections in the Museum of Fine Arts,* Boston, 1930.

Dani, A.H., *Indian Paleography,* Oxford University Press, 1963.

Deming, W.E., *Sample Design in Business Research,* John Wiley and Sons, New York, 1960.

Denzin, Norman, *The Research Act,* Aldine, Chicago, 1973.

Ebeling, Claus, *Ragamala Painting,* Kumar Gallery, New Delhi, 1973.

Emory, C.W. and D.R. Cooper, *Business Research Methods,* Richard D. Irwin, Homewood, Illinois, 1991.

Fisher, R.A., *The Design of Experiment,* Oliver and Boyd, Edinburgh, 1937.

Floyd, J.F., *Survey Research Methods,* Sage Publications, New Delhi, 1993.

Fox, David J., *The Research Process in Education,* Holt, Rinehart and Winston, New York, 1993.

Ganguli, O.C., *Ragas and Raginees,* Rupam, Banaras, 1936.

Gosh, M.H., *An Introduction to Research Procedure in Social Sciences,* Asia Publishing House, Bombay, 1964.

Glock, C.Y., *Survey Research in Social Sciences,* Russel Sage Foundation, New York, 1967.

Goods, Carter V. and Douglas E. Scates, *Methods of Research,* Appleton Century Crofts, New York, 1954.

Goode, William J. and P.K. Hatt, *Methods in Social Research,* McGraw Hill, New York, 1952.

Gopal, M.H., *An Introduction to Research Procedure in Social Sciences,* Asia Publishing House, Bombay, 1970.

Guha, J.P., *Introducing Indian Art,* R and K. Publishing House, New Delhi, 1963.

Havell, E.B., *The Art Heritage of India,* D.B. Taraporevala Sons and Co. Pvt. Ltd., Bombay, 1964.

Hillway, T., *Introduction to Research,* University of Chicago Press, Chicago, 1975.

Hyman, Herbert H., *Interviewing in Social Research,* University of Chicago Press, Chicago, 1975.

Katz, W.K., *Introduction to Reference Work,* McGraw Hill, New York, 1987.

Kerlinger, F.N., *Foundations of Behavioural Research,* Holt, Reinhart and Winston Inc., USA, 1998.

Khandalavala, Karl, *Brief Survey of Indian Painting,* New Book Co., Bombay, 1958.

———, *Development of Style in Indian Painting,* Macmillan, New Delhi, 1969.

Krathwohl, David R., *How to Prepare Research Proposal,* Syracuse University Bookstore, Syracuse, New York, 1976.

Krishna, C., *History of Indian Painting, Mughal and Deccan Tradition,* Abhinav Publications, New Delhi, 1979.

Krishna Rao, M.V.N., *Indian Script Deciphered,* Agam Kala Prakashan, New Delhi, 1984.

Kumar, K., *Research Methods in Library and Information Science,* Har-Anand Publications, New Delhi, 1992.

Leedy Paul, D., *Practical Research: Planning and Design,* Macmillan, New York, 1980.

Lundberg, G.A., *Social Research: A Study in Methods of Gathering Data,* Longman, Green and Co., New York, 1929.

Mill, John Stuart, *A System of Logic,* Longmans, New York, 1930.

Miller, D.C., *Handbook of Research Design and Social Measurement,* David McKay Company, Inc., New York, 1977.

Misra, R.P., *Research Methodology,* Concept Publishing Company, New Delhi, 1989.

Murthy, R.S.S., *Introduction to Manuscriptology,* Sharda Publishing House, Delhi, 1996.

Oppenheim, A.N., *Questionnaire Design and Attitude Measurement,* Basic Books, New York, 1966.

Parten, Mildred, *Surveys, Polls and Samples, Practical Procedures,* Harper, New York, 1950.

Powell, T.G.E., *Prehistoric Art,* Praeger Publishers, Inc., USA, 1966.

Ramachandran, P., *Training in Research Methodology in Social Sciences in India,* ICSSR, New Delhi, 1971.

Randhawa, M.S., *Indian Miniature Painting,* Roli Books International, New Delhi, 1981.

Robert, G. Murdik and Donald R. Cooper, *Business Research: Concepts and Guides,* Columbus, Ohio, Grid, 1982.

Rosenburg, Morris, *Logic of Survey Analysis,* Basic Books, New York, 1968.

Salkind, N.J., *Exploring Research,* Prentice Hall, New Jersey, 1991.

Selltiz, C., M. Jahoda, M. Deutsch and S.W. Cook, *Research Methods in Social Relations*, Holt, Reinhart and Winston, Inc., USA, 1961.

Sidney, Elizabeth and Margret Brown, *Skills of Interviewing,* Tavistock Publication, London, 1961.

Srivastava, G.N.P., *Advanced Research Methodology,* Radha Publications, New Delhi, 1994.

Sukhia, L. and C. Malhotra, *Elements of Educational Research,* Allied Publishers, Bombay, 1960.

Tandon, B.C., *Research Methodology in Social Sciences,* Chaitanya Publishing House, Allahabad, 1987.

Traverse, R.M.W., *An Introduction to Educational Research,* Macmillan Publishing Company, Inc., New York, 1978.

Vaidya, K.L., *Pahadi Chitrakala,* National Publishing House, Delhi, 1969.

Vishwakarma, R.K., *Bhartiya Chitrakala Mein Sangeet Tatva* (Hindi), Publications Division, Ministry Information and Broadcasting, GOI, New Delhi, 1996.

Vatsyayan, Kapila, *Dance in Indian Painting,* Abhinav Publications, New Delhi, 1981.

Waldschmidt, E., and R. Leonore, *Miniatures of Musical Inspiration,* Popular Prakashan, Bombay, 1967.

Whitney, F.L., *The Elements of Research,* Prentice Hall, Inc., New York, 1954.

Wilkinson, T.S. and P.L. Bhandarkar, *Methodology and Techniques of Social Research,* Himalaya Publishing House, Bombay, 1979.

Yates, F., *Sampling Methods for Censuses and Surveys,* Macmillan, New York, 1981.

Young, Pauline V., *Scientific Social Surveys and Research,* Prentice Hall, New York, 1949.

Index